STEAK FRITES

AND CLASSIC FRENCH BISTRO COOKING

STEAK FRITES

AND CLASSIC FRENCH BISTRO COOKING

PIERRE-YVES CHUPIN

6th avenue books

6th avenue books™ are published by:

AOL Time Warner Book Group
1271 Avenue of the Americas
New York, N.Y. 10020

Visit our Web site at www.twbookmark.com

An AOL Time Warner Company

First Printing 10 9 8 7 6 5 4 3 2 1

ISBN: 1-931722-21-8

This book was produced and designed by
Quintet Publishing Limited
6 Blundell Street
London N7 9BH

Senior Project Editor: Corinne Masciocchi
Editor: Anna Bennett
Art Director/Designer: Simon Daley
Photographer: Juliet Piddington
Food Stylist: Kathryn Hawkins
Creative Director: Richard Dewing
Publisher: Oliver Salzmann

Manufactured in Singapore by PICA Digital (Pte) Ltd.
Printed in China by Leefung-Asco Printers Ltd.

CONTENTS

INTRODUCTION

Steak frites, a simple but classic combination of steak and fries which captures the very essence of French bistro cooking, is one of the leading dishes of this important gastronomic tradition, of which the French are stalwart defenders.

Bistro: the very word has an appealing ring to it. Some people believe it to be derived from the Russian word "bistro," meaning "quickly," which the Cossacks who arrived in Paris in 1814 used to shout out to waiters in order to hurry up the service. Bistros proper first appeared in the early 20th century, with the arrival in Paris of people from the Auvergne region, the Bougnats, who tried to make a living first as coal merchants and later as café proprietors. They could always find a bit of space at their stalls to prepare a few *plats du jour* and to give people a taste of their local produce. Roquefort cheese, Puy lentils, and tripe: culinarily speaking, Paris was thus transformed into something of an outpost of the Auvergne. Today the bistro business is still the mainstay of the Auvergnats, and the best establishments are divided among a few great families from this region.

While bistros were beginning to appear in Paris, France's individual regions remained faithful to their own customs and their particular specialties. Produce did not travel very well at that time and cooking was dictated by whatever fresh ingredients were locally available. Each village had its own cook, who was sent for on special occasions. Engagements, christenings, and weddings provided the only opportunities for feasting in this rural way of life. Restaurants as such were not commonly known in those days, but the rapid development of the railways gradually made it necessary to set up premises where travelers could obtain refreshments. After a few decades the French national menu was drawing its inspiration from the entire rail network. The Railway Restaurant, or Railway Hotel, became a veritable gastronomic institution, and was found more or less everywhere.

After World War II, when people traveled more frequently by automobile, a further gastronomic explosion occurred. Auberges sprang up all along the *routes nationales*, and especially those leading south. Joigny, Saulieu, Vienne, and Valence in particular became unmissable stops on this gastronomic tour. No motorist would leave the house without his Michelin guide, which listed not only the addresses of garages but also of selected eating places. The proprietors quickly became prosperous thanks to these modern-day travelers. The first paid holidays heralded the dawn of the leisure culture, and there was no question of forgoing the pleasures of fine fare along the way.

At every stop, the menu invited travelers to discover and share in the fine produce of the area, and they came to demand genuine, authentic regional specialties. They wanted to see the chef dressed in traditional costume,

INTRODUCTION

swapping his chef's hat for a Basque beret. He would, typically, rise early in the morning to pick herbs, pick mushrooms, or hunt wild boar. From now on meals would be prepared from just such a collection of local delicacies. Through the network of stopping-places, gourmet France took shape and grew into a mosaic of tastes and flavors, of local specialties and variations. The desire for modern comforts (which was very often influenced by customs abroad) in no way dimmed French regionalism but, on the contrary, prompted its resurgence on the menu and gave it a new lease of life.

Different parts of France all have their own different culinary tradition. Lyons, for example, revered its *mères*, although these female proprietors owed no allegiance to any particular group and did not champion any particular gastronomic style. *Mères* were cooks, formerly employed in bourgeois households, who quickly became enthusiastic restaurateurs. Their establishments embodied a kind of permanence, which defined the town and presented it to the outside world as the capital of fine fare. Mères Rijean, Brazier, and Filloux, to mention just a few, could make unparalleled quenelles, chicken in vinegar, and chicken stuffed with truffles. On a more modest level, Lyons also had its *bouchons*, originally places where the staff gave the horses a rub down (*bouchonner*) while the traveler went to get his meal. In these modest establishments the proprietors offered very nourishing dishes and snacks that were enjoyed particularly by the local silk workers. In these popular, crowded eating places customers could sample a wide choice of cold or hot pork dishes, potato salads, or lentils, all washed down with Beaujolais. On the strength of both its *bouchons* and its

mères, Lyons was not obliged to pledge any allegiance to Paris. While the capital was turning out more and more bistros and brasseries serving thousands of dishes each day, Lyons favored a simpler style of cooking and had little tolerance for the over-sophisticated style of Parisian waiters and maîtres d'hôtel. To further develop its own style, Lyons sent out for supplies from all the surrounding regions: the Dombe for pike, Bresse for poultry, and Beaujolais for wine. In this way the town managed to remain confident enough to preserve its own culinary traditions.

Parisian culinary fashions fared no better further east, in the cuisine of Strasbourg and Alsace as a whole. The people of Alsace have always had great appetites, and a good meal often serves as a business card in this region. Although it has endured food shortages, famine, and war in its history, this region has always maintained a consistent love of feasts. Whether the cuisine is popular, peasant, or bourgeois matters little. Christian or secular festivals are all accorded their range of specialities, particularly charcuterie and patisserie. Gingerbread is baked for the feast of St. Nicholas, and there are special dishes for the feast of St. Hubert (the patron saint of hunters) and of St Vincent (the patron saint of grape-pickers); whatever the event or the date, it seems the important thing here is to have a feast. And it is very much in the *winstub* (literally "wine bar") that the exuberance of Alsace finds an outlet and best expresses itself. In the vineyards that cover a large part of the plain of Alsace, every village has its own winstub. In these hostelries, which are always very reliable, the cuisine revolves around feast days, and consequently also around the seasons. At the start of the hunting or fishing

season therefore, or of the grape harvest, the menu of the day will include a fillet of pike-perch, some venison, or a meat pie made with Riesling. The traditional Sauerkraut is the hallmark dish in Alsatian taverns, where the beer flows freely, as is the impressive Tarte flambée—a cream cheese, onion, and bacon tart (*see* page 16) traditionally prepared by housewives on Monday, washday, and cooked in the baker's oven—and many pork-based specialties.

Besides Lyons and Strasbourg, two regional capitals that have shown great initiative in competing to establish their cuisine within the national heritage, rural France also boasts a successful culinary reputation. The whole of the southwest, from Bordeaux to the Basque country, from Périgord to the Languedoc, is a veritable land of milk and honey. This region must have been no

stranger to hardship, however, since throughout history it has always tried to find ways to store food, to preserve, to bottle fruit, and make conserves. Was it fear of famine, or anxiety about the future, which turned the art of cooking here into the art of survival? Every season brought its own tasks: pigs to be slaughtered, fruit and vegetables to be harvested, mushrooms to be picked, geese or ducks to be force-fed in order to store up resources and provide for the days to come. And tucked away in every cellar, securely protected from daylight, heat, and above all from greedy eyes, were impressive stores: lampreys, truffle sauces, or conserves. It is easy to see how the cuisine of the southwest, where the fruits of nature were stored with such care and attention, would eventually spread to the outside world. The reputation of the produce, the

INTRODUCTION

beauty of the landscape, and the mild climate all contributed to attract lovers of good food to the region's country inns and restaurants. There had to come a day when the proprietor of the village café was moved to offer them his pâtés, his terrines, or a little of his wonderful Rustic country soup (*see* page 65) which was simmering by the fireside. The southwest and its auberges, often run by women, became increasingly accessible by train, by car, or even by bicycle: henceforth the whole of gourmet society could converge on this culinary El Dorado.

It has to be acknowledged that neighboring countries, and in particular Britain, have helped the French to return to their roots. Since the early twentieth century, wealthy tourists, especially those who spent their summers in Nice, Biarritz, or Dinard, have enjoyed exploring the many different surrounding routes, with the pleasant prospect of a good meal, perhaps enjoyed outdoors, at some picturesque bistro. The tradition persists, and the smart set from abroad still enjoy such simple pleasures along the roads of France.

The arrival of nouvelle cuisine in the 1970s, far from ruining these establishments or effacing their customs, on the contrary gave them a new lease of life. In the restaurants listed in the guides or by the famous reviewers, the food became ever more minimalist, and the cooking sought to glorify the finest and often the most unusual produce, but the French as well as the foreign tourists appreciated it when they came across a bistro, an inn, or other *bouchon* which still served generous portions of food which was simply prepared but highly flavored and colorful. Society changes, and eating habits with it. Every day, the slate which takes place of pride in the middle of the room and lists the menu provides some solace and a little bit of self-indulgence in this ever more demanding world. Uniformity and dullness have no place here: there is a day for a Sea bream à la Niçoise (*see* page 46), a day for Duck parmentier (*see* page 62), and one for a Navarin of spring lamb (*see* page 80) accompanied through the week by the salad of herring and potatoes with oil, the house terrine, the bowl of chocolate mousse or the inevitable tart made from whatever fruit is in season. In the face of such a successful return to the old favorites, perceptive chefs have been keen to take the plunge themselves and open their own bistros. For minor cooks and great chefs alike, the test is the same: to get the best from what the seasons have to offer, to create enjoyable and tempting dishes from cuts or produce which are not particularly special in themselves. So the bistro need not be in awe of its great and distant past. It has shown itself able to adapt to our everyday life, which provides its very *raison d'être*. Bistro fare nowadays eschews fat, encourages the consumption of vegetables and fish, and is moderate in its use of sugar. We are fortunate that the bistro has still not been consigned to a museum. It has become more essential than ever in a country which has always taken great pleasure in food and which delights, at every change in the season, in the appearance of a new menu.

Pierre-Yves Chupin

GLOSSARY

BEAUFORT CHEESE A full-flavored, alpine, semi-hard cheese similar to Gruyère. It is matured for 18 months to produce a fruity, nutty flavor and a smooth, creamy, buttery paste. A whole cheese weighs up to 130 pounds (60 kg) and has a distinctive concave edge.

BOUQUET GARNI A bunch of herbs tied together and used for flavoring soups and stews. The classic bouquet garni consists of one sprig of thyme, one sprig of parsley, and two bay leaves. Other herbs are frequently added such as rosemary, savory, sage, basil, celery leaves, chervil, and tarragon. Ready-made bouquets garnis are available in food stores.

COMTÉ CHEESE A hard, aromatic cheese from the Franche-Comté region. Flavors vary from nutty, to fruity and piquant yet sweet, depending on the age of the cheese. If unavailable, substitute with Emmenthal or Gruyère.

CONFIT A specialty from southwest France, confit is a preserved food item, usually a meat like duck, goose, or pork. The meat is salted and cooked slowly in its own fat. It is then transferred into a pot and covered with the cooking fat which acts as a seal and preservative. It is bought ready-made in glass jars or cans.

FOIE GRAS A great French delicacy, foie gras is the liver of a specially fattened goose or duck. It is available either as a whole liver whereby entire lobes are prepared in a cloth, terrine, or jar, or simply poached in vacuum-packing. This type of foie gras is the most expensive and best served on its own to fully appreciate its delicate flavor. Regular foie gras (pieces of liver lobe massed together), is the cheaper version and therefore perfect as a cooking ingredient. It is also readily available in terrines, jars, cans, or vacuum packing.

FROMAGE BLANC A mild-flavored, creamy, soft cheese that has not been ripened. Made with whole or skimmed milk and cream, it has the consistency of cream cheese, but with fewer calories. It can be bought in tubs, but if unavailable, low-fat cream cheese is an acceptable substitute.

GRUYÈRE CHEESE A semi-soft cheese originating from Switzerland, and readily available in supermarkets. Slightly grainy, it has a wonderful complexity of flavors—at first fruity, it becomes more earthy and nutty with age.

LIVAROT CHEESE A semi-soft, full-flavored, pungent, slightly piquant cheese from Normandy. If unavailable, substitute with Pont l'Évêque.

MOREL MUSHROOMS Morel mushrooms have short, thick, hollow stems, topped with sponge-like pointed caps. They can be tan, yellow, or black in color and produce a rich, nut-like flavor and fragrance.

PASTIS Also known as Pernod or Ricard, Pastis is a licorice-flavored liqueur. It is the direct descendant of the infamous absinthe, the favorite drink of *fin de siècle* Paris.

REBLOCHON A soft, creamy, slightly salty cheese from the Savoy region in southeast France. If unavailable, use Brie or Monterey Jack instead.

SAUTERNES A sweet, white dessert wine made in the southern Bordeaux district of France.

TOURNEDOS is a very lean cut of beef about 1-inch ($2\frac{1}{2}$-cm) thick and $2\frac{1}{2}$ inches ($6\frac{1}{2}$ cm) in diameter that has been cut from the tenderloin.

VIN JAUNE A dry, white food wine from the Jura region which is yellow in color, hence its name which translated literally means "yellow wine." The wine is aged in oak barrels for a minimum of six years. As it ages, the color becomes bright yellow, the bouquet develops a surprising strength, and despite its 13 or 14 degrees, the taste of walnut continues to develop.

1 APPETIZERS

POIVRONS MARINÉS

Bell peppers with garlic and capers

A dish that is often served in summer in the country restaurants of Provence and all around the Mediterranean coast. Broiling the peppers and removing the skins helps to remove any bitterness.

SERVES 4 • 40 MINUTES PREPARATION + 6 HOURS MARINATING • 20 MINUTES COOKING

3 large red bell peppers

3 large yellow bell peppers

1 medium head garlic

1¼ cups (10 fl. oz/300 ml) olive oil

Salt and fresh ground black pepper

1 tablespoon capers

1 Preheat the oven broiler. Line a dripping pan with foil. Place the oven shelf in the center of the oven and position the dripping pan just underneath.

2 Place the red and yellow bell peppers, whole, on the shelf. Brown them, turning frequently so that the skin blisters evenly. When they are well-browned, remove from the oven and transfer them immediately to a plastic bag. Seal the bag and allow the bell peppers to cool. The skins will then be very easy to peel off.

3 Preheat the oven to 350 °F (180 °C).

4 Peel the garlic cloves and cut into slivers. Place in a small baking dish, and add the olive oil. Cover with a sheet of foil and place in the preheated oven for about 20 minutes, checking frequently. The garlic should be well cooked and lightly colored. Reserve the olive oil. Allow to cool in the dish.

5 As soon as the bell peppers have cooled, remove the skins and stems. Cut into halves and remove the white parts. Cut the bell peppers into strips and rinse under cold water to remove all seeds. Dry thoroughly with paper towels. Place them in a baking dish, taking care to arrange the different colors pleasingly.

6 Season sparingly with salt and pepper, and add the capers. Add the garlic and cover with the olive oil from the baking dish. Marinate in the refrigerator for at least 6 hours.

7 Remove the dish from the refrigerator 1 hour before serving. Sprinkle with black pepper to serve.

WINE A Provence rosé (Côtes de Provence or Bandol)

TARTE FLAMBÉE

Alsatian cream cheese, onion,
and bacon tart

In Alsace, this tart was traditionally cooked in the baker's oven, so it is important to have an oven that heats to a high temperature for rapid, effective cooking. Fromage blanc is the fresh cheese that would be used in France to make this tart. If this is unavailable, substitute with cream cheese or ricotta.

SERVES 8 • 30 MINUTES PREPARATION • 2 MINUTES COOKING

9 oz (250 g) bread dough

2 lb, 4 oz (1 kg) fresh cheese, such as fromage blanc, cream cheese, or ricotta

3⅛ cups (25 fl.oz/750 ml) crème fraîche

1 tablespoon all-purpose flour

Pinch of salt

1 tablespoon vegetable oil

10½ oz (300 g) bacon, cubed

4 medium onions, chopped

2 tablespoons salted butter

Pinch of nutmeg

Fresh ground black pepper

1 Preheat the oven to 475 °F (240 °C).

2 Roll out the dough as thinly as possible and use it to line a large oblong cookie sheet 16 x 12 inches (40 x 30 cm). Prick the dough base with a fork and bake blind for 10 minutes then allow to cool for about 10 minutes. Do not turn off the oven.

3 To make the cheese topping, combine the fresh cheese, crème fraîche, flour, salt, and oil to form a thick paste and spread it over the dough using a wooden spatula.

4 Brown the bacon in a skillet.

5 Peel and chop the onions and brown them in the butter.

6 Scatter the bacon and onions over the cheese topping. Season with a pinch of nutmeg and some pepper, return to the oven, and cook for 2 minutes.

WINE A white Alsace wine (Riesling or Gewurztraminer)

Tarte flambée

TERRINE DE DINDE

Turkey terrine

A terrine should be kept for a few days before eating: the flavors will blend together and the meat will become more tender. Seal the terrine with a luting paste made with all-purpose flour and a little water. Roll the resulting paste into a sausage shape, which you can wrap around the lid to seal it. To make this recipe, you will need a proper ceramic or glazed cast-iron terrine dish with a lid.

SERVES 8 • 35 MINUTES PREPARATION • 1¾ TO 2 HOURS COOKING

2 lb, 4 oz (1 kg) boneless turkey, sliced

Salt and fresh ground black pepper

9 oz (250 g) pork

9 oz (250 g) bacon

9 oz (250 g) veal

9 oz (250 g) ham

2 teaspoons allspice

2 medium eggs

1 shot glass Cognac

10 bacon slices

1½ cups (5 oz/150 g) all-purpose flour

⅓ cup (3½ fl. oz/100 ml) water

1 Season the turkey slices with salt and pepper. Set aside.

2 Dice the pork, bacon, veal, and ham. Mix thoroughly in a bowl.

3 Season the meat mixture with salt, pepper, and allspice. Add the eggs and Cognac. Mix thoroughly to blend all the ingredients.

4 Line a 10 x 5-inch (25 x 12-cm) terrine dish with 5 bacon slices. Spread a layer of the meat mixture on top of the bacon followed by a layer of turkey slices. Repeat and finish with a layer of the meat mixture. Top with the remaining bacon slices.

5 Place the lid on the terrine dish and make a luting paste by mixing the flour and water together. Roll into a sausage shape and use this to seal the edges of the lid so that the terrine is airtight.

6 Place the terrine dish in a roasting pan half-filled with hot water, and cook in the oven for 1¾ to 2 hours.

WINE A white Burgundy (Chablis or Bourgogne Aligoté)

FOIE GRAS POÊLÉ AUX RAISINS

Fried duck foie gras with grapes

For some years, bistros have taken to serving fried foie gras. It is delicious with apples, quince, or figs, which should first be browned for a few minutes in a little butter or duck fat.

SERVES 6 • 25 MINUTES PREPARATION • 10 MINUTES COOKING

1 uncooked duck foie gras weighing 1 lb, 5 oz to
1 lb, 12 oz (600 g to 800 g)

2 to 3 tablespoons all-purpose flour

Salt and fresh ground black pepper

1 small bunch white grapes

4 slices white bread (from a sandwich loaf)

⅔ cup (5 fl. oz/150 ml) Sauternes, or sweet white wine

Few sprigs chervil, to garnish

1 Working diagonally across, slice four good thick escalops from the foie gras. Using a small knife, remove any nerves you can reach without damaging the escalops. Dust with flour and shake to remove any excess. Season and keep cool.

2 Wash the grapes and use the point of a knife to remove the skin and pips. Toast the slices of bread on one side only so as not to dry them out, and set aside.

3 Heat a nonstick skillet over a high heat (do not use any fat or oil) and brown the escalops for 1 minute on each side. Remove from the skillet, place on paper towels, and keep warm.

4 Deglaze the pan with the Sauternes, add the grapes, and cook for 3 minutes until the liquid has reduced. Place one slice of toast on each plate, top with an escalop, decorate with the grapes, and coat with the sauce. Serve immediately, garnished with chervil.

WINE A very sweet wine (Sauternes, Loupiac, Quarts-de-Chaume, or Bonnezeaux)

SOUPE DE POISSONS

Fish soup

This soup, admittedly time-consuming to prepare, can more than hold its own alongside the famous bouillabaisse of Marseilles. The result is delicious, and well worth the effort. If you like, add a little saffron at the end and serve the soup topped with a little rouille sauce.

SERVES 4 • 30 MINUTES PREPARATION • 1¼ HOURS COOKING

1 medium leek

4 medium cloves garlic

1 large onion

2 lb, 4 oz (1 kg) assorted fish (conger eel, gurnard, red mullet, John Dory, etc.)

½ cup (3½ fl. oz/100 ml) olive oil

4 medium tomatoes

4 sprigs thyme

1 bay leaf

Salt and fresh ground black pepper

Olive oil, for frying

4 slices rough grain country bread

Pinch of saffron strands, optional

1 Clean the leek and chop coarsely. Peel and chop the garlic and onion.

2 Rinse the fish and cut into pieces.

3 In a pot gently cook together the leek, garlic, and onion in the olive oil. Cut the tomatoes into eight wedges and add to the pot along with the thyme and the bay leaf.

4 Add the fish and cover with 3 quarts (3 l) cold water. Bring to a boil and simmer gently for 1 hour.

5 Remove the fish from the pot and discard the skins, heads, and bones. Discard the bay leaf and return the flesh to the soup for another 15 minutes.

6 When cooled, put the soup through a vegetable mill to purée. Season and reheat, adding the saffron strands if using.

7 Meanwhile, fry the bread in a little olive oil and keep ready to serve with the soup.

WINE A white wine from Provence (Cassis or Côtes de Provence)

SALADE DE POMMES DE TERRE AUX MOULES

Potato salad with mussels

It is important to choose waxy potatoes, such as Charlotte, or Pompadour for this traditional salad. Serve lukewarm or chilled.

SERVES 4 • 30 MINUTES PREPARATION • 30 MINUTES COOKING

8 medium waxy potatoes

2 lb, 2oz (1 kg) mussels

Scant 1 cup (7 fl. oz/200 ml) dry white wine

Pinch of saffron strands

1 small celery stalk, including the leaves

½ cup (3½ fl. oz/100 ml) crème fraîche

1 tablespoon Dijon mustard

2 tablespoons olive oil

1 tablespoon sherry vinegar

8 sprigs flat-leaf parsley

Salt and fresh ground black pepper

1 Peel and wash the potatoes and steam for 20 to 25 minutes, or place in a saucepan of cold salted water, bring to a boil, and cook for 20 to 25 minutes.

2 Meanwhile, scrub the mussels, removing all beards and barnacles. Discard any that do not close when tapped sharply. Place the mussels in a casserole dish with the white wine and cook over a high heat for a few minutes until they open. Discard any that fail to open.

3 Strain the mussel liquor and add the saffron. Allow to soak.

4 Remove the mussels from their shells.

5 Peel the celery and chop it finely. For the cream sauce, mix the crème fraîche, mustard, oil, and vinegar in a bowl. Set aside. Finely chop the parsley.

6 When the potatoes are done, cut into slices and place in a salad bowl. Sprinkle them with the mussel liquor while they are still hot, and mix together well. Add the mussels, celery, cream sauce, and chopped parsley. Season and mix together thoroughly.

WINE Muscadet

SOUFFLÉS AU BEAUFORT

Soufflés with Beaufort cheese

The béchamel sauce can also be made by adding the milk a little at a time to a very slightly browned roux. These soufflés are also excellent made with other cheeses: Comté, Cantal, Cheddar, Parmesan, or blue cheeses such as Fourme d'Ambert.

SERVES 4 • 25 MINUTES PREPARATION • 20 MINUTES COOKING

4 oz (120 g) Beaufort or Gruyère cheese

½ stick (4 tablespoons) salted butter

⅓ cup (1¼ oz/40 g) all-purpose flour

1 cup (8 fl. oz/250 ml) milk

Salt and fresh ground black pepper

Pinch of nutmeg

4 medium eggs

Fresh grated Parmesan cheese, for dusting

1 Set aside a small piece of the Beaufort (about ¾ oz/20 g) and grate the rest. Slice the small piece into shavings using a potato peeler.

2 Melt three quarters of the butter in a saucepan. Add the flour and cook, stirring continuously with a spatula or a whisk. When the mixture is lightly browned, add all the milk at once, bring to a boil, then remove from the heat, continuing to stir vigorously. Add the seasoning and a pinch of freshly grated nutmeg.

3 Carefully separate the eggs and beat the whites until stiff peaks form. Away from the heat, add the yolks and the grated Beaufort to the contents of the saucepan, then add the egg white, folding it in carefully with a metal spoon so as not to lose any air.

4 Preheat the oven to 350 °F (180 °C).

5 Butter four individual 4-inch (10-cm) diameter soufflé dishes with the remaining butter, dust with the Parmesan cheese, and tap the bases to shake out the excess. Fill three-quarters full with the mixture and dot the surface with the shavings of Beaufort.

6 Place in the oven for 20 minutes. Do not open the door during cooking, and serve the soufflés immediately after removing from the oven, so they do not collapse.

WINE White wine from the Jura (Arbois or Côtes du Jura)

FILETS DE ROUGETS FLAMBÉS AU PASTIS

Red mullet flambéed with Pastis

At her bistro in Saint-Illide, Catherine Guerraz likes to pay homage in her cooking to her native south. This colorful recipe is especially easy to prepare and can be made at the last minute.

SERVES 4 • 30 MINUTES PREPARATION • MULLET 8 TO 10 MINUTES COOKING

4 red mullet, filleted

Salt and fresh ground black pepper

3 medium cloves garlic

Olive oil, for frying

14 oz (400 g) fresh tagliatelle pasta

8 cherry tomatoes, halved

8 pitted black olives

¼ cup (2 fl. oz/50 ml) Pastis or Pernod

Few basil leaves

1 Ask your fish merchant to fillet the red mullet. Season the fillets and slice them in half.

2 Peel and crush the garlic.

3 Heat a little olive oil in a skillet over a gentle heat. Add the garlic and the fish fillets (skin-side up) and allow to cook for 8 to 10 minutes.

4 Meanwhile, cook the tagliatelle until *al dente*. When cooked, place a portion of tagliatelle on each plate and arrange the mullet on top.

5 Place the skillet in which the mullet were cooked back on the stove, this time over a high heat. Add the tomatoes, olives, and the pastis. Carefully ignite the pastis to flambé, scraping the bottom of the skillet with a wooden spoon to incorporate all the cooking juices.

6 When the flames have died down, pour the sauce over the mullet, sprinkle with a few chopped basil leaves, and serve immediately.

WINE A rosé wine (Côtes de Provence)

BROUILLADE AUX POINTES D'ASPERGES

Scrambled eggs with asparagus tips

Scrambled eggs can also be made in a double-boiler, adding almost all of the butter, in pieces, to the egg and asparagus mixture, and reserving the Parmesan for flavoring the asparagus tips after dipping them briefly in the remaining butter.

SERVES 4 • 15 MINUTES PREPARATION • 30 MINUTES COOKING

1 lb, 2 oz (500 g) green asparagus

6 large eggs

½ stick (4 tablespoons) salted butter

⅔ cup (5 fl. oz/150 ml) crème fraîche

Salt and fresh ground black pepper

3 tablespoons grated Parmesan cheese

1 Peel the asparagus using a vegetable peeler then cut off the bases of the stalks and any woody parts. Cut off the tips to a length of about 2 inches (5 cm).

2 Bring a large saucepan of salted water to a boil. Wrap the tips in a cloth or place them in a small colander. This is done so that they can easily be removed from the pan later on. Throw in the asparagus stalks and the tips.

3 After 5 minutes, take out the asparagus tips, refresh in cold water, and set aside.

4 Allow the asparagus stalks to cook for a further 10 minutes, drain thoroughly, and squeeze out the excess water before using a blender to purée.

5 Beat the eggs lightly in a bowl with a fork then add the asparagus purée. Melt the butter in a skillet and cook the egg and asparagus mixture over a very gentle heat, stirring constantly with a wooden spatula.

6 When the eggs start to set and you can see the base of the saucepan, gently add the crème fraîche. Season with salt and pepper and add the Parmesan. When the scrambled eggs are ready, place the asparagus tips on top to reheat them briefly and turn off the heat so that the scrambled eggs stay soft and light. Serve immediately.

WINE A white Alsace wine (Riesling or Gewurztraminer)

PÂTÉ EN CROÛTE

Pork and veal pie

A great classic of French gastronomy. Making a slit in the pastry allows the steam to escape during cooking, preventing the pie from bursting. For special occasions, a few truffle shavings may be added to the filling.

SERVES 8 • 40 MINUTES PREPARATION • 2 HOURS COOKING

1 lb 2 oz (500 g) pork

1 lb 2 oz (500 g) stewing veal

9 oz (250 g) ham

Salt and fresh ground black pepper

14 oz (400 g) puff pastry

10 bacon slices

1 medium egg yolk

FOR THE FILLING

7 oz (200 g) ham, diced

7 oz (200 g) sausage meat

4 oz (125 g) button mushrooms, halved

5 shallots, peeled and sliced thin

Sprig of thyme, chopped

Parsley, chopped

1 medium egg

1 shot glass **Cognac**

Salt and fresh ground black pepper

1 Cut the pork, veal, and ham into slices. Season and set aside.

2 Prepare the filling by mixing together all the filling ingredients.

3 Roll out the puff pastry, keeping a piece to one side for covering the pie. Line a large 10 x 5-inch (25 x 12-cm) ovenproof dish with the pastry, allowing it to overlap the edges.

4 Arrange 5 bacon slices over the base. Cover with alternating layers of filling and slices of meat, ending with a layer of the remaining bacon slices.

5 Fold the overlapping pastry over the top of the dish. Cover the pie with the puff pastry you have kept aside. Seal with a little beaten egg yolk and pinch the pastry together with your fingers.

6 Using a sharp knife, make a slit in the middle to act as a vent.

7 Brush the top of the pastry evenly with some egg yolk to glaze. Cook for 2 hours in a moderate oven (375 °F/190 °C).

WINE A white Burgundy (Meursault or Montrachet)

PÂTÉ AUX POMMES DE TERRE

Potato pie

This pie can also be served as a main course, along with a green salad garnished with a few finely chopped shallots.

SERVES 6 • 30 MINUTES PREPARATION • 1 HOUR COOKING

4 shallots

1 lb 10 oz (750 g) potatoes

Salt and fresh ground black pepper

Pinch of nutmeg

1 sheet ready-rolled pastry dough

1 cup (8 fl. oz/250 ml) crème fraîche

7 oz (200 g) Comté, Emmenthal or Gruyère cheese, grated

1 sheet ready-rolled puff pastry

1 medium egg yolk

1 Preheat the oven to 375 °F (190 °C).

2 Peel and thinly slice the shallots. Peel, wash, and dry the potatoes. Cut them into thin slices. In a bowl, mix together the potatoes and shallots. Add the seasoning and nutmeg, and mix thoroughly.

3 Place the pastry dough in a 10-inch (25-cm) round buttered pie pan, allowing it to overlap the dish slightly.

4 Place half of the potatoes and shallots on the pie base. Spread them out, then coat with half of the crème fraîche, followed by half of the grated cheese. Repeat to make a second layer.

5 Unroll the puff pastry and place over the top of the dish, cutting off the excess. Seal the edges with the overlapping pastry dough, pinching regularly between your fingers, moistened with cold water. Using a sharp knife, make a slit in the middle and insert a strip of foil wound around itself several times as a funnel. This will enable the steam to escape during cooking. Score the surface of the puff pastry using a sharp knife.

6 Dilute the egg yolk with a little water to make a glaze. With a pastry brush, generously coat the top of the pie. Place in the oven for 1 hour, covering with foil to prevent over-browning. Serve very hot.

WINE A Loire white wine (Sancerre or Menetou-Salon)

TERRINE AUX FOIES DE VOLAILLE

Chicken liver terrine

This is the most classic of all terrines, and perhaps the most flavorful. It is important to cook the terrine in a double boiler to avoid it drying out and to obtain a smooth, creamy texture.

SERVES 8 • 30 MINUTES PREPARATION • 1¼ HOURS COOKING

10½ oz (300 g) chicken livers

½ cup (4 fl. oz/100 ml) Port

1 sprig rosemary

2 bay leaves

5½ oz (150 g) bacon

6 tablespoons salted butter

1 teaspoon allspice

Salt and fresh ground black pepper

Toasted French bread, sliced thin

Herbs of your choice, to garnish

1 Place the chicken livers in a dish and cover them with the Port, rosemary, and bay leaves. Cover and marinate for 1 hour in a cool place.

2 Preheat the oven to 350 °F (180 °C).

3 Cut the bacon into small pieces and plunge them into a saucepan of boiling water for 5 minutes. Drain and mix with the livers, marinade, butter, allspice, and salt and pepper to make a purée.

4 Turn this purée into a buttered 10 x 5-inch (25 x 12-cm) terrine dish. Place the dish in a roasting pan half-filled with hot water and cook in a preheated oven for 1¼ hours.

5 Remove from the oven, allow to cool, and refrigerate overnight before eating. Serve with toasted bread and a herb garnish.

WINE A Loire red (Saumur-Champigny or Chinon)

SALADE DE ROSEVAL
AUX ANCHOIS

Potato salad with anchovies

This salad should be served well chilled. It is advisable to prepare it at least two hours before serving, so the shallots can blend into the sauce.

SERVES 4 • 30 MINUTES PREPARATION • 30 MINUTES COOKING

3½ oz (100 g) anchovies in salt or oil

8 medium waxy potatoes, such as Charlotte, Belle de Fontenay, or Pompadour

½ cup (4 fl. oz/100 ml) dry white wine

2 shallots, sliced thin

2 tablespoons capers

FOR THE VINAIGRETTE

4 tablespoons olive oil

1 tablespoon wine vinegar

Salt and fresh ground black pepper

8 sprigs parsley, chopped fine

1 If the anchovies are salted, soak them for 1 hour in a small bowl of cold water to remove the salt.

2 Peel and wash the potatoes and place in a saucepan of cold salted water, bring to a boil, and cook for 20 to 25 minutes.

3 Meanwhile, drain the anchovies, slice the fillets into halves down the middle, and remove the bones.

4 When the potatoes are done, cut into slices and place in a bowl. While still warm, sprinkle them with the white wine, which will prevent them from absorbing too much oil afterward, and mix well.

5 Add the shallots to the potatoes together with the anchovies and capers.

6 Make a vinaigrette by mixing together the olive oil, vinegar, salt, and pepper. Pour over the potatoes. Sprinkle with the chopped parsley and mix thoroughly.

WINE A white wine from Languedoc-Roussillon (Côtes du Roussillon)

Salade de roseval aux anchois

ŒUFS EN MEURETTE

Baked eggs in red wine sauce

A traditional recipe from Burgundy, which should be served with rustic country bread and butter, or on slices of bread fried in a little garlic butter, to mop up the delicate, fragrant sauce.

SERVES 4 • 30 MINUTES PREPARATION • 1 HOUR COOKING

2 tablespoons salted butter

¼ cup (1 oz/25 g) all-purpose flour

1½ cups (12 fl. oz/350 ml) red wine

1 bouquet garni (*see* **Glossary, page 12**)

1 onion, sliced thin

3 shallots, sliced thin

Salt and fresh ground black pepper

8 large eggs

1 Preheat the oven to 350 °F (180 °C). Blend the butter and flour together in a casserole over very low heat, making sure that the flour does not brown. Then add the wine, a small glass of water, the bouquet garni, and the sliced onion and shallots. Season and allow to simmer over a very low heat for 1 hour.

2 Remove from the heat, strain, and fill four ramekin dishes two-thirds full with the sauce. Break two eggs in each ramekin and bake for a few minutes in the oven so that the yolks remain soft. Remove from the oven, season with pepper, and serve with fresh bread.

WINE A red Burgundy (Savigny-lès-Beaune or Hautes Côtes de Nuits)

CRÈME DE CAROTTES AU CUMIN

Carrot and cumin soup

Made with fresh, flavorful carrots, this easily prepared soup has a delightfully sweet flavor. Try it and see; your guests will ask for more!

SERVES 4 • 15 MINUTES PREPARATION • 30 MINUTES COOKING

8 medium carrots (1 lb/450 g)

1 cup (8 fl. oz/250 ml) full-fat crème fraîche

1 teaspoon ground cumin

Salt and fresh ground black pepper

1 Wash and peel the carrots, and cut them into chunks.

2 Place the carrots in a large pot and cover with water. Bring to a boil and simmer for 30 minutes.

3 Remove the carrots from the pot and place them in a mixing bowl. Add the crème fraîche, the cumin, and a quarter of the cooking water. Mix well.

4 Season and serve lukewarm or cold.

QUICHE AUX ASPERGES ET SAUMON

Asparagus and salmon quiche

When baking the pastry for the pie crust, it is a good idea to cover it with a circle of waxed paper and fill it with either baking beans, rice, or garbanzo beans (or, better still, with cherry pits kept for the purpose) so that it keeps its shape and does not buckle. Remove the paper and baking beans, rice, or garbanzo beans when the pie crust is cooked.

SERVES 6 • 35 MINUTES PREPARATION • 55 MINUTES COOKING

10½ oz (300 g) pastry dough

Butter, for greasing

1 lb, 2 oz (500 g) asparagus tips

5½ oz (150 g) smoked salmon

3 medium eggs

1 cup (8 fl. oz/250 ml) crème fraîche

1 tablespoon Dijon mustard

1 cup (8fl. oz/250 ml) milk

Salt and fresh ground black pepper

1 Roll out the pastry and use it to line a buttered pie pan. Prick the pastry and bake blind for 10 minutes in a hot oven (425 °F/220 °C).

2 Meanwhile, peel the asparagus, discarding most of the tough stem and reserving the tips and the tender parts. Cook for 15 minutes in boiling salted water. Drain on paper towels and chop roughly.

3 Fill the cooked pie crust with the chopped asparagus and strips of smoked salmon.

4 In a bowl, beat together the eggs, cream, mustard, milk, salt, and pepper.

5 Pour the mixture into the pie shell and bake in a moderate oven (375 °F/190 °C) for 30 minutes.

WINE A white Loire wine (Anjou or Vouvray)

TOURTE AU LIVAROT

Livarot cheese pie

A specialty of Normandy, which can also be made with any other cheese from that region such as Pont l'Évêque. Serve with a green salad seasoned with a light dressing.

SERVES 4 • 20 MINUTES PREPARATION • 40 MINUTES COOKING

⅔ **cup (5 fl. oz/150 ml) milk**

¾ **oz (12 g) baker's yeast**

2¼ **cups (9 oz/250 g) cake flour**

1 medium egg

½ **stick (4 tablespoons) salted butter, softened, plus extra for greasing**

Pinch of salt

½ **Livarot cheese or Pont l'Évêque**

Scant 1 cup (7 fl. oz/200 ml) crème fraîche

Salt and fresh ground black pepper

Green salad, to serve

1 Warm the milk. In a separate bowl, mix the yeast with a few spoonfuls of the milk. Add the flour, egg, butter, and a pinch of salt. Knead the dough, then transfer to a floured work surface. Roll into a ball, flatten it out with the palm of your hand, then gather it up into a ball again. Roll out the dough.

2 Grease a 9-inch (23-cm) pie dish with butter and, using the rolling pin, lift up the dough and use it to line the pie dish. Cover with a dish towel and allow to rise for 1 hour in a warm place.

3 Preheat the oven to 300 °F (150 °C).

4 Remove the rind from the cheese and cut it into thin slices.

5 Arrange the slices of cheese on the dough base and spread the cream on top using the back of a spoon. Season with salt and pepper.

6 Bake for 40 minutes, until the top is golden brown.

7 Remove the pie from the oven, allow to stand for 5 minutes, then turn it out and cut into generous portions. Serve hot with a green salad on the side.

TO DRINK Dry cider

2 FISH

MORUE À LA SAVOYARDE

Salt cod with onions and potatoes

An easy dish, which should be prepared the day before serving to ensure all the salt is removed from the cod. For extra flavor, sprinkle a little grated Beaufort or Gruyère cheese over the fish, onions, and potatoes just before baking.

SERVES 6 • 30 MINUTES PREPARATION + OVERNIGHT SOAKING • 40 MINUTES COOKING

2 lb, 12 oz (1.2 kg) salt cod

3 small onions

Olive oil, for frying

12 medium potatoes

1 tablespoon all-purpose flour

Fresh ground black pepper

Lemon wedges and chopped parsley, to garnish

1 The day before you plan to serve the dish, place the cod in a sieve immersed in a basin of cold water, ensuring that the fish does not touch the bottom of the basin. Change the water several times while the cod is soaking.

2 The following day, when you are ready to cook the cod, preheat the oven to 400 °F (200 °C). Peel the onions, slice them into fine rings, and cook in olive oil over a low heat until golden. Take care not to burn them.

3 Carefully wash the potatoes, place in a saucepan, and cook in boiling water until done. Drain, remove the skins, and cut into round slices about ½ inch (1 cm) thick.

4 Heat sufficient olive oil in a skillet to fry the potato slices and fry over gentle heat until golden.

5 Add the onions to the potatoes, cover the skillet, and continue to cook over a gentle heat.

6 Lift the cod from the soaking water, drain, and cut into large pieces. Lightly flour and, in a separate skillet, fry until golden over a high heat.

7 Combine the cod with the potatoes and onions. Place all the ingredients in an ovenproof dish and cook for 10 minutes in a preheated oven.

8 Remove from the oven, season generously with pepper, and serve immediately, garnished with lemon wedges and chopped parsley.

WINE A white wine from Savoy (Roussette or Chignin-Bergeron)

MAQUEREAUX AU VIN BLANC

Mackerel in white wine

Use a dry white wine, preferably a Muscadet, for this recipe. The mackerel can be served as a simple but delicious appetizer, as is the custom in Brittany, accompanied by slices of fresh white bread and salted butter.

SERVES 4 • 25 MINUTES PREPARATION • 20 MINUTES COOKING

2 medium onions

2 small carrots

2 unwaxed lemons, sliced

1 tablespoon olive oil

2 sprigs rosemary

2 sprigs thyme

1 bay leaf

2 cloves

2 mackerel, cleaned and gutted

⅔ cup (5 fl. oz/150 ml) dry white wine

Salt and fresh ground black pepper

1 Peel and slice the onions and carrots. Cut the lemons into slices. Heat the oil in a skillet, then lightly brown the carrots, onions, the slices from one of the lemons, one rosemary and one thyme sprig, the bay leaf, and cloves for 5 minutes.

2 Add the mackerel and cover with the wine. Season and cook for 15 minutes over a gentle heat.

3 Remove from the heat and arrange the mackerel on a serving dish using the remaining lemon slices as a garnish.

4 Strain the cooking liquor and pour over the mackerel.

5 Allow to cool completely before serving. Garnish with the remaining rosemary and thyme sprigs.

WINE Muscadet

ROUGETS AU FOUR À L'HUILE D'OLIVE

Baked red mullet in olive oil

This dish works best in summer, when tomatoes are beautifully ripe. You could also use two dozen flavorful cherry tomatoes, cut in half. Use only the best-quality olive oil to dress the dish—a good olive oil with a slightly lemony aroma is particularly good with fish. Ask your fish merchant to fillet the red mullet for you.

SERVES 4 • 20 MINUTES PREPARATION • 20 TO 25 MINUTES COOKING

6 medium tomatoes

2 unwaxed lemons

1 medium head garlic

Scant 1 cup (7 fl. oz/200 ml) olive oil

1 red mullet weighing 2 lb, 12 oz to 3 lb, 5 oz (1.2 kg to 1.5 kg), filleted

8 bay leaves

2 to 3 sprigs thyme

Salt and fresh ground black pepper

1 Preheat the oven to 350 °F (180°C).

2 Remove the skin and seeds from the tomatoes. Cut into large pieces. Wash the lemons by scrubbing them gently. Cut into fine slices. Break up the head of garlic without removing the skin from the cloves.

3 Use some of the olive oil to oil a gratin dish slightly larger than the fish. Place the fish fillets in it and arrange the garlic, tomato chunks, and lemon slices around it. Insert the bay leaves between the garlic, tomato, and lemon slices. Sprinkle with half of the remaining olive oil. Scatter the thyme over the entire dish and add a little salt.

4 Place in the oven and cook for 20 to 25 minutes, depending on the size of the fillets.

5 Remove from the oven. Arrange the fillets on four warmed plates. Place the vegetables around the fish and pour over the juices. Sprinkle with a little salt and pepper, and drizzle generously with the remaining olive oil to serve.

WINE A white wine from Provence or the Languedoc-Roussillon area

TURBOT SAUCE BÉARNAISE

Turbot with béarnaise sauce

Béarnaise sauce can be difficult to get right. If you follow this recipe carefully, however, you should have no problems. This sauce also goes well with other quality fish or rare joints of meat.

SERVES 4 • 40 MINUTES PREPARATION • 30 MINUTES COOKING

Salt and fresh ground black pepper

1 turbot weighing about 3 lb, 5 oz (1.5 kg)

1 tablespoon olive oil

2 shallots

2 tablespoons fresh chopped tarragon

½ cup (4 fl. oz/100 ml) white wine vinegar

2 medium egg yolks

1 stick (8 tablespoons) salted butter

1 Season and rub the turbot all over with olive oil.

2 Place the fish under the broiler with the dark skin side uppermost, about 8 inches (20 cm) below the flame.

3 Cook for about 15 minutes, then turn the fish over and continue cooking for 15 minutes more.

4 Meanwhile, peel and chop the shallots. Place them in a heavy-based saucepan with 1 tablespoon of tarragon.

5 Cover with the vinegar and reduce to two thirds over a gentle heat. Remove the saucepan from the heat and strain the juices, pressing well in order to extract all the flavoring.

6 Put the egg yolks and 2 tablespoons butter in another saucepan, and gradually add the strained juices while whisking thoroughly. Place this saucepan over a double boiler of gently simmering water and continue to whisk until the mixture starts to thicken.

7 Now add the remaining butter, cut into small pieces, to the sauce. Continue to whisk throughout. Season, add the remaining chopped tarragon, then pour into a gravy boat.

8 Carefully remove the dark skin from the turbot and serve immediately with the sauce.

WINE A good white wine from the Rhône valley (Hermitage or Châteauneuf-du-Pape)

BROCHET BEURRE BLANC

Pike in white butter sauce

White butter sauce (beurre blanc) is one of the great classics of French cuisine. A good tip to help you to make this well-known sauce successfully is to add a tablespoon of crème fraîche just before the butter. To ensure the fish is very hot before you serve it, soak it for a minute or so in the remaining broth.

SERVES 4 • 40 MINUTES PREPARATION • 30 MINUTES COOKING

2 medium carrots

1 medium leek

Salt and fresh ground black pepper

¾ cup (6 fl. oz/175 ml) dry white wine

½ bunch parsley

2 cloves

4 sprigs thyme

2 bay leaves

1 pike weighing about 3 lb, 5 oz (1.5 kg)

FOR THE WHITE BUTTER SAUCE

5 shallots, chopped fine

1 tablespoon white wine vinegar

Fresh ground black pepper

2 sticks (16 tablespoons) very cold salted butter

1 To make the fish broth, peel the carrots, wash these and the leek, then chop. Place the chopped vegetables in a fish kettle, cover with water, season, bring to a boil, and cook for a few minutes. Add the white wine, parsley, cloves, thyme, and bay leaves, and bring to a boil once more. Turn off the heat and allow the broth to cool in the fish kettle.

2 Carefully lower the pike into the cold broth. Bring to a boil and cook for 15 minutes after the first bubbles begin to appear.

3 Remove from the heat and gently lift out the pike. Keep warm. Strain the broth.

4 To make the white butter sauce, put the chopped shallots, the white wine vinegar, and 1 scant cup (7 fl. oz/200 ml) of the strained fish broth in a saucepan. Add pepper and reduce the liquid by at least two thirds over a high heat.

5 Reduce the heat and add the butter a little at a time, whisking continuously. Strain the sauce and serve immediately.

WINE A dry white Anjou (preferably Savennières)

DAURADE À LA NIÇOISE

Sea bream à la Niçoise

A traditional recipe, brought back to our tables by the great French chef Jacques Maxim. The bread slices absorb the sauce during cooking and are really delicious!

SERVES 4 • 20 MINUTES PREPARATION • 30 MINUTES COOKING

4 slices French bread

1 large clove garlic, peeled

1 sea bream weighing about 2 lb, 4 oz (1 kg)

½ cup (4 fl. oz/100 ml) olive oil

1 stick (8 tablespoons) salted butter

½ cup (4 fl. oz/100 ml) lemon juice

2 medium tomatoes, diced

20 black olives, pitted

Rock salt and fresh ground black pepper

5 basil leaves, chopped, to garnish

1 Preheat the oven to 350 °F (180 °C). Rub the bread slices with the garlic clove to flavor.

2 Place the sea bream in an ovenproof dish. Add ½ cup (4 fl. oz / 100 ml) water, the olive oil, butter, lemon juice, diced tomatoes, olives, and bread slices. Season with rock salt and pepper and cook in the oven for 30 minutes.

3 Remove the dish from the oven. Reserve the liquor, whisk vigorously, and pour into a gravy boat. Serve the fish with the sauce, and garnish with the chopped basil leaves.

WINE A white wine from the Mediterranean coastal region (Cassis or Côtes de Provence)

MOULES AUX POIVRONS

Mussels with bell peppers

An unusual way of cooking mussels. Serve with thick slices of crusty bread fried in salted butter or olive oil.

SERVES 4 • 25 MINUTES PREPARATION • 10 MINUTES COOKING

2 lb, 2 oz (1 kg) mussels

1 small head garlic

1 medium red bell pepper

1 medium green bell pepper

1 tablespoon olive oil

3 bay leaves

3 sprigs thyme

1 bunch curly parsley, chopped fine

1¼ cups (10 fl. oz/300 ml) dry white wine

Salt and fresh ground black pepper

1 generous piece salted butter

Chopped parsley, to garnish

1 Scrub the mussels, removing all beards and barnacles. Discard any that do not close when tapped sharply. Remove the skin from the garlic cloves. Wash and dice both bell peppers.

2 Heat the olive oil in a large flameproof casserole dish. When the oil is hot, add the garlic, bay leaves, thyme, parsley, and diced bell peppers, and cook over a high heat for 5 minutes.

3 Add all the mussels to the casserole dish without lowering the temperature, leaving the dish uncovered. Pour in the white wine. Stir thoroughly for another 5 minutes. Add a little salt. Remove the casserole from the heat and lift out the mussels, keeping them hot in a serving dish. Discard any mussels that have failed to open.

4 Strain the mussel liquor and pour into a saucepan, bringing to a boil in order to reduce the liquor by about one third. Add the butter a little at a time, whisking continuously. Season with pepper. Pour the sauce over the mussels and sprinkle with chopped parsley to garnish. Serve immediately.

WINE Muscadet

Moules aux poivrons

MORUE À LA CRÈME

Salt cod baked in cream

This is an old country recipe for salt cod. Make sure you cut the potatoes as thinly as possible to make cooking easier.

SERVES 4 • 25 MINUTES PREPARATION• 1 HOUR COOKING

1 lb, 10 oz (750 g) salt cod

6 medium potatoes

1 medium onion

1 sprig thyme

1 bay leaf

1 clove garlic

Salt and fresh ground black pepper

1 cup (8 fl. oz/250 ml) crème fraîche

½ cup (4 fl. oz/100 ml) milk

1 The day before you plan to cook the salt cod, soak it in a bowl of water making sure that you change the water at regular intervals.

2 The day of cooking, peel the potatoes and cut them into thin round slices.

3 Bring a saucepan of water to a boil with the peeled onion, thyme, and the bay leaf. Add the cod and poach for 5 minutes. Remove the cod from the pan, drain it, and in a bowl, gently break it up without mashing it.

4 Rub a gratin dish all over with the garlic clove. Make a layer of potatoes then a layer of cod. Add a little salt and pepper and repeat the layers until you have used all up the ingredients.

5 Mix the crème fraîche with the milk and pour over the fish and potatoes. Place in a hot oven and cook for 1 hour.

WINE Chablis

ANDOUILLETTES DE BAR

Stuffed sea bass roulades

This recipe is delicious and surprisingly easy to make.
Ask your fish merchant to fillet the sea bass for you.
Serve with sautéd potatoes or fries.

MAKES 10 • 1 HOUR PREPARATION • 5 MINUTES COOKING

1 medium leek

1 large, flat mushroom

1 medium carrot

1 medium onion

2 tablespoons salted butter

3⅓ oz (3½ oz/100 g) white fish meat

Salt and fresh ground black pepper

1 large egg

½ cup (3½ fl. oz/100 ml) crème fraîche

1 sea bass weighing about 6 lb, 8 oz (3 kg)

FOR THE SAUCE

½ tablespoon dried fish broth (available in supermarkets)

3 shallots, peeled and chopped

2 tablespoons salted butter

1 tablespoon crème fraîche

1 tablespoon wholegrain mustard

1 tablespoon chives, chopped fine

1 Peel and wash the vegetables. Slice the leek and mushroom thinly. Peel and slice the carrot and onion thinly, and fry for a few minutes in a saucepan with the butter, making sure they remain crisp. Drain thoroughly and set aside.

2 In a blender, mix the white fish meat with the salt and pepper. Add the egg, mix, then gradually add the crème fraîche, mixing all the time. Finally, add the drained vegetables and mix thoroughly. Set this mixture aside.

3 Cut some foil into 10 sheets, about 8 x 10 inches (20 x 25 cm) in size. Butter two thirds of the nonshiny side.

4 Using a sharp knife, cut the filleted sea bass into thin slices. To make the roulades, arrange one or two fillets in the center of each buttered foil sheet so that they cover two thirds of the sheet. Using two tablespoons, arrange a little of the fish meat and vegetable mixture in a sausage shape in the center of each fillet. Wrap the fillet around the mixture, then wrap it all in the foil sheet, twisting the foil at either end like a candy wrapping.

5 Place the roulades in a large saucepan of boiling salted water for 5 minutes.

6 Meanwhile, make the sauce. Dilute the fish broth in 1 cup (8 fl. oz/250 ml) water. Sweat the shallots in the butter. Add the crème fraîche, fish broth, mustard, and chives, and bring to a simmer.

7 Take the fish roulades out of the water, remove from the foil, and serve with the sauce.

WINE Chablis

3 MEAT AND POULTRY

POULET À L'ESTRAGON

Chicken with tarragon sauce

It is recommended that a very dry white wine, such as Muscadet, be chosen for this recipe: its acidity will give a bit of sharpness to the cream. This classic dish is traditionally served with rice, but leaf spinach or fondant potatoes go just as well.

SERVES 4 • 30 PREPARATION • 50 MINUTES COOKING

1 whole chicken weighing 3 lb, 5 oz (1.5 kg)

½ stick (4 tablespoons) salted butter

3 tablespoons all-purpose flour

½ cup (4 fl. oz/100 ml) white wine

Salt and fresh ground black pepper

1 medium onion

2 cloves

4 sprigs tarragon

½ cup (4 fl. oz/100 ml) crème fraîche

2 medium egg yolks

1 Joint the chicken into four pieces. Brown the chicken pieces in the butter in a skillet. When they are golden-brown, sprinkle with the flour. Stir well to make sure the flour is cooked then moisten with the white wine and ½ cup (4 fl. oz/ 100 ml) water. Season. Add the whole onion studded with the cloves, and 2 sprigs of tarragon. Bring to a boil, then reduce the heat, cover, and cook for 45 minutes.

2 Take the chicken out of the skillet, reserving the cooking juices. Transfer to a serving dish, and keep hot. Discard the onion.

3 Whisk the cream and egg yolks in a bowl. Chop one tarragon sprig. Mix the reserved cooking juices into the cream and egg yolk mixture, add the chopped tarragon, then pour the contents of the bowl into the skillet and stir well. Gently heat the sauce without allowing it to boil and adjust the seasoning to taste. Coat the chicken with the tarragon sauce and serve garnished with the remaining tarragon sprig.

WINE A white wine from the Rhône Valley (Saint-Joseph or Crozes-Hermitage)

STEAK FRITES

Steak with French fries

Steak Frites is a true bistro classic. Serve in its purest form, or, for a bit of a kick, serve with a pepper sauce. You can use black peppercorns, but the French use green peppercorns as this adds a touch of piquancy and punch to the dish.

SERVES 4 • 20 PREPARATION • 25 MINUTES COOKING

FOR THE FRENCH FRIES

4 large potatoes

Vegetable oil, for deep-frying

Sea salt, to season

FOR THE PEPPER SAUCE

4 tablespoons Cognac

4 tablespoons green or black peppercorns, lightly crushed

2 tablespoons salted butter

⅔ cup (5 fl. oz/150 ml) crème fraîche

Salt, to season

4 fairly thick fillet beef steaks weighing a total of 1 lb, 9 oz (700 g)

1 Start by making the fries. Peel and rinse the potatoes. Cut them into thick slices, then cut into "fries".

2 In a heavy-based, high-sided skillet suitable for deep-frying, heat sufficient vegetable oil in which to fry the potato fries to 350 °F (180 °C).

3 Cook the fries in batches. Place a small quantity of fries in a frying basket and deep-fry for 10 minutes, until golden-brown and crisp. Drain the basket and empty the fries onto a tray lined with paper towels. Repeat, allowing the oil to heat up between cooking one batch of fries and the next.

4 Sprinkle the drained fries with sea salt and keep warm.

5 To cook the steaks, heat the butter in a skillet and brown the steaks for 3 minutes each side over a high heat. Season to taste and serve immediately.

6 If you are opting for the pepper sauce, pour the Cognac into a soup plate and soak each steak on both sides for a few seconds. Reserve the Cognac.

7 Put the lightly crushed peppercorns in a dish and place each steak in the pepper on both sides, pressing lightly so that the pepper sticks to the meat.

8 Heat the butter in a skillet and brown the steaks for 3 minutes each side over a high heat. Pour in the Cognac and carefully set alight to flambé.

9 When the flames have died down, remove the steaks from the skillet and keep warm. Discard the cooking butter and return the skillet to a high heat. Pour in the cream and bring to a boil, scraping the bottom of the skillet thoroughly with a wooden spoon to incorporate all the cooking juices. Season and pour the sauce over the steaks.

WINE A red Burgundy or Beaujolais

CANARD AUX POIRES

Duck with pears

Pears and celeriac always go well together. They enhance the flavor of fowl, especially duck, particularly well. Serve the duck with French beans.

SERVES 6 • 45 MINUTES PREPARATION • 40 MINUTES COOKING

Salted butter, for melting

1 duck, jointed into 6 pieces

6 small pears

1 celeriac

Juice of 1 lemon

Salt and fresh ground black pepper

Few sprigs chervil, to garnish

1 Preheat the oven to 425 °F (220 °C).

2 Melt a knob of butter in a casserole dish and brown the duck on all sides. Remove the duck and set it aside. Reserve the juices left in the casserole.

3 Peel the pears and cut into quarters. Brown them in the casserole dish with the cooking juices from the duck.

4 Peel the celeriac and cut into slices. Put the slices in boiling water for 3 minutes.

5 Add the celeriac slices in the casserole dish with the pears, the duck, and the lemon juice. Season.

6 Place in the oven and cook for 40 minutes. Serve with the cooking juices spooned over and garnish with sprigs of chervil.

WINE Bordeaux or a Loire red (Chinon or Bourgueil)

POULET AUX GOUSSES D'AIL

Chicken with garlic

A particularly good way of preparing chicken, as the chicken can take its time to cook and the meat just melts in the mouth. A recipe which Catherine Guerraz, in her country bistro in Saint-Illide, France, likes to serve with small braised potatoes.

SERVES 4 • 30 MINUTES PREPARATION • 1½ HOURS COOKING

1 cup (4½ oz/125 g) all-purpose flour

Salt and fresh ground black pepper

1 free-range chicken weighing 3lb, 5 oz (1.5 kg)

2 sprigs of thyme

5 bay leaves

2 tablespoons olive oil

5 heads of garlic

1 Put the flour in a bowl, make a well and add half a glass of water a little at a time. Blend together with the fingertips to make a ball of pastry. Cover and leave to rest.

2 Preheat the oven to 200 °C (390 °F).

3 Season the inside of the chicken and put in the sprigs of thyme and the bay leaves.

4 Using a pastry brush, coat the chicken inside and out with olive oil. Put the chicken in a cast-iron casserole dish with the unpeeled heads of garlic.

5 Place the lid on the casserole and seal it by wrapping the strip of pastry around the lid.

6 Place in the oven and cook for 1½ hours.

7 Remove from the oven, break off the pastry seal and serve at once with small braised potatoes.

WINE A red Côtes-du-Rhône (Saint-Joseph or Cornas)

Poulet au citron

POULET AU CITRON

Chicken with lemon

To enhance the aroma of the lemon, add a little grated rind to the sauce. Use a very aromatic pepper, such as Szechuan pepper.

SERVES 4 • 10 MINUTES PREPARATION • 1¼ HOURS COOKING

Juice and rinds of 2 lemons

4 medium onions

1 chicken weighing about 3 lb, 5 oz (1.5 kg)

Salt and fresh ground Szechuan pepper

2 sprigs thyme

2 tablespoons salted butter

3 sprigs cilantro

Lemon wedges and sprigs of thyme, to garnish

1 Preheat the oven to 400 °F (200 °C).

2 Squeeze the lemons and reserve the rinds. Peel the onions and quarter each of them.

3 Season the chicken cavity with salt and pepper and stuff it with one of the chopped onions, the lemon rinds, and the sprigs of thyme.

4 Put the chicken in a casserole dish, pour the lemon juice over it, and dot it with small medallions of butter. Surround it with the remaining onions and two of the cilantro sprigs. Put the lid on the casserole and place it in the oven.

5 Allow to cook for 1¼ hours, removing the lid after 1 hour to allow the chicken to brown a little. Turn off the heat but leave the chicken in the oven for 10 minutes, with the lid half off.

6 Remove the chicken and cut into pieces. Serve seasoned with salt and ground pepper surrounded by the onions. Garnish with lemon wedges, sprigs of thyme, and the remaining cilantro sprig. Strain the cooking juices and serve in a gravy boat.

WINE A white Bordeaux (Graves or Pessac-Léognan)

DAUBE DE PINTADE

Guinea fowl casserole

The chocolate strengthens the flavor of the sauce to great effect. Choose something simple like pasta or polenta to go with this dish, then you can enjoy the rich sauce without feeling guilty!

**SERVES 4 • MARINATE OVERNIGHT •
40 MINUTES PREPARATION • 2¼ HOURS COOKING**

1 guinea fowl weighing 3 lb (1.3 kg)

1 large carrot

2 cloves

1 large onion

5½ oz (150 g) celery

1 bouquet garni (*see* **Glossary**, page 12)

5 black peppercorns

Pinch of allspice

4 cups (36 fl. oz/1 l) red wine, preferably **Côtes-du-Rhône**

24 small onions

5½ oz (150 g) bacon

3 tablespoons all-purpose flour

2¼ oz (60 g) goose or duck fat

Salt and fresh ground black pepper

¾ oz (10 g) semisweet chocolate

1 Ask your butcher to joint the guinea fowl into pieces. Peel and finely slice the carrot. Push the cloves into the onion, then trim the celery and chop it into pieces. Mix all these ingredients in a bowl, add the bouquet garni, the peppercorns, and a pinch of allspice. Moisten with the red wine. Allow the guinea fowl pieces to marinate in this mixture overnight in the refrigerator.

2 The day of cooking, peel the small onions but keep them whole, and cut the bacon into small cubes. Remove the guinea fowl from the marinade, drain, dry carefully on paper towels, and dust lightly with flour, shaking off the excess. Heat the marinade gently in a saucepan without allowing it to boil.

3 Preheat the oven to 300 °F (150 °C).

4 Brown the bacon pieces and the small onions in the goose or duck fat in a casserole dish. When they are well-browned, remove them and brown the pieces of guinea fowl in the same way on all sides for 10 minutes. Return the onions and bacon to the casserole dish. Moisten with the marinade, season, cover, and cook in the oven for 2 hours.

5 Remove and discard the bouquet garni and the clove-studded onion, take out a ladleful of the sauce, melt the chocolate in it, pour it back into the casserole and stir it in, taking care not to break up the guinea fowl pieces.

WINE A red wine from southwest France (Cahors or Buzet)

GIGOT D'AGNEAU EN GIBIER

Lamb with game marinade

A novel way to cook lamb, leaving it for a whole day in a well-flavored marinade as is done with game. A good winter's dish, which is even better when re-heated. So don't hesitate to increase the quantities and keep some for the next day or the one after.

SERVES 6 TO 8 • 45 MINUTES PREPARATION • 1 HOUR 25 MINUTES COOKING

1 leg of lamb weighing about 6 lb, 7oz (3 kg)

3 medium carrots

2 medium leeks

2 medium onions

2 bouquets garnis (*see* **Glossary**, page 12)

10 medium whole cloves of garlic

10 peppercorns

4½ cups (34 fl. oz/1 l) dry white wine

2 large glasses of white Port

30 small white onions

3 heads of celeriac

1 tablespoon lemon juice

Salted butter, for frying

FOR THE MOREL SAUCE

9 oz (250 g) dried morel mushrooms

2¼ cups (17 fl. oz/500 ml) crème fraîche

1 The previous day, ask the butcher to bone the lamb but to leave the bone in. Put the lamb in a large container with the carrots, the white parts of the leeks, the onions, 1 bouquet garni, and 5 whole garlic cloves which should not be peeled but crushed a little. Add the peppercorns, cover with the wine and Port. Allow the lamb to soak in this marinade. At the same time (the previous day) soak the dried morels in cold water.

2 The day of cooking, take the lamb out of the marinade. Cook the marinade gently for 30 minutes, then pass it through a sieve. Peel the small white onions, blanch them for 5 minutes, and drain. Brown the lamb well on all sides in oil in a large casserole dish, add the small onions, a fresh bouquet garni, and 5 fresh peeled cloves of garlic. Cook uncovered for 1 hour, basting with marinade from time to time. Reduce the marinade to two thirds in a pan (having kept back a little for basting the meat), blend in the crème fraîche, and reduce gently for 10 minutes. This sauce should be nice and smooth. Then add the washed, drained morels, cook for 5 minutes, and keep in a warm place.

3 Peel the celeriac heads and dice into large pieces. Cook them for 20 minutes in boiling salted water with the lemon juice. Drain and sauté in butter. Add a little parsley.

4 When the lamb is cooked, remove it from the casserole, drain, transfer to a large dish, and remove the bone from the center simply by pulling it out. Carve into slices, cover with the morel sauce, and serve with the sautéed celeriac.

WINE A white from the Jura, or a red Burgundy

PARMENTIER DE CANARD

Duck Parmentier

Hachis Parmentier is a dish normally made with beef, but here the beef is replaced by duck, which reigns supreme in the southwest of France. It is featured in many recipes, along with the traditional confits that are made in the region. These are conserves made with duck, goose, pork, or poultry giblets that are first salted, then cooked slowly and preserved in their rendered fat. Serve this dish with a green salad dressed with walnut oil.

SERVES 6 • 30 MINUTES PREPARATION • 1 HOUR 40 MINUTES COOKING

2 shallots

1 medium carrot

1 small celery stalk

2 tablespoons oil

1 small **Barbary** or similar duck, jointed

3 cups (24 fl. oz/750 ml) dry white wine

1 bouquet garni (*see* **Glossary**, page 12)

2 medium cloves garlic, peeled and minced

Salt and fresh ground black pepper

One 9-oz (250-g) piece duck confit (*see* **Glossary**, page 12)

2 lb, 4 oz (1 kg) potatoes

½ stick (4 tablespoons) salted butter

1 Peel and thinly slice the shallots. Peel and slice the carrot. Trim and finely chop the celery stalk.

2 Heat the oil in a casserole dish on the stove and brown the duck pieces on both sides, adding the shallots, carrot, and celery after a few minutes.

3 Pour in the white wine and 1 cup (8 fl. oz/250 ml) water, add the bouquet garni, the minced garlic, and salt and pepper. Cook for 1 hour over a gentle heat, until the flesh of the duck comes away easily from the bones.

4 Brown the piece of duck confit in a saucepan, beginning on the side with the skin. Do not let the confit dry out, but let it sweat out as much fat as possible.

5 Wash the potatoes and put them in a large saucepan; cover them with cold water, bring to a boil, then lower the heat and cook for 25 to 30 minutes, depending on their size.

6 Preheat the oven to 425 °F (220 °C). Butter a gratin dish with 2 tablespoons butter.

7 When the duck is done, remove from the casserole, and continue to reduce the liquid over a gentle heat.

8 Remove and discard the skin and bones from the duck pieces and chop the flesh. Remove and discard the skin and fat from the confit, chop it up, and mix it with the duck, the confit serving as a kind of binding agent.

9 When the potatoes are cooked, drain, peel, and put them through a food processor to reduce them to a purée.

10 Remove the fat and sieve the cooking liquid from the duck using a strainer.

11 Spread half the purée in the gratin dish, then spread the chopped duck in a layer on top. Pour on a few spoonfuls of the cooking liquid, but not too much.

12 Cover with the remaining purée and dot the surface with the remaining butter, cut in small pieces.

13 Place the gratin dish in the center of the oven and allow it to brown for 30 minutes.

14 Serve hot, straight from the oven.

WINE A Bordeaux or a red wine from the southwest of France (Cahors or Gaillac)

GARBURE

Rustic country soup

This hearty, wholesome soup is served as a main course. If you cannot find a ham bone, you can add a heel of dried ham instead, preferably slightly aged. When fava beans are not in season, replace them with fresh, small, white navy beans, and in winter with dried beans, though you will have to soak and cook them separately before adding them to the soup. You will need 2 lb, 4 oz (1 kg) unshelled fava beans to obtain the shelled weight required for the recipe. For extra flavor, you can rub a clove of garlic onto your bread or even, as the French do, add a glass of red wine to the soup.

SERVES 8 • 30 MINUTES PREPARATION • 1 HOUR COOKING

1 small **Savoy** cabbage

4 small carrots

2 medium turnips

1 medium leek

4 medium potatoes

4 medium cloves garlic

1 ham bone

2 sprigs thyme

1 bay leaf

Salt and fresh ground black pepper

14 oz (400 g) fresh fava beans, shelled weight

8 confit duck or goose legs (*see* **Glossary**, page 12)

8 slices country bread, toasted

1 Wash the cabbage, carrots, turnips, leek, and potatoes. Peel those that need peeling, then cut them into chunks. Strip the leaves off the cabbage, remove the hard part from the sides, and cut the green part into strips.

2 Put the above vegetables into a stockpot along with garlic, ham bone, thyme, and bay leaf. Cover with water, add salt and pepper, and cook for 1 hour, uncovered, on a rolling boil. Add water if necessary but the soup must remain thick.

3 Half an hour before cooking is finished, add the beans and the confit duck legs, having first removed any excess fat from them.

4 Arrange the slices of toasted bread in the bottom of a soup tureen and pour the soup over them. Serve steaming hot.

WINE Bordeaux or a red wine from the southwest of France (Madiran)

POT AU FEU DE FOIE GRAS

Poached foie gras with vegetables

A great recipe for special occasions, and not at all difficult to prepare. For an added touch of luxury, add a little finely grated truffle just before serving.

**SERVES 4 • 30 MINUTES PREPARATION •
ABOUT 45 MINUTES COOKING**

8 small carrots carrots

8 small turnips

4 medium leeks

8 small onions

8 small potatoes

8 leaves green cabbage

1 cooked duck or goose foie gras weighing about 1 lb, 5 oz (600 g)

3 chicken broth cubes

½ cup (4 fl. oz/120 ml) Port

½ cup (4 fl. oz/120 ml) Madeira

Salt and fresh ground black pepper

1 Peel and wash the vegetables, and keep them whole. Prepare the foie gras, removing any traces of green left by the gall bladder.

2 Bring 6¼ cups (50 fl. oz/1.5 l) water to a boil with the broth cubes in a large saucepan and boil the carrots, turnips, leeks, and onions. Remove from the heat and keep warm in the saucepan. Cook the potatoes separately in salted water.

3 Blanch the cabbage leaves in boiling salted water in a saucepan for a few minutes. Drain and set aside.

4 Pour the Port and Madeira in another saucepan and add two thirds of the chicken broth in which the vegetables were cooked. Bring to a boil and allow to reduce slightly. Then reduce the heat so that the liquid is barely simmering, put in the foie gras, and cook for about 15 minutes. Carefully remove the foie gras with the aid of a skimming ladle and wrap it in a dish towel to dry.

5 Using a sharp knife, cut the foie gras into eight slices about ¾ inch (1 cm) thick. Season each slice and wrap in a cabbage leaf.

6 Transfer the foie gras-filled cabbage leaves to a serving plate and surround with the vegetables. Strain the foie gras cooking liquor through a conical strainer and pour this broth over the foie gras and vegetables.

WINE Bordeaux

BŒUF AU VIN ROUGE

Beef in a chestnut glaze with red wine shallot sauce

Devised by the top chef at The White Barn Inn in Maine, the unusual combination of ingredients works really well together.

SERVES 4 • 1 HOUR PREPARATION • 40 MINUTES COOKING

7 oz (200 g) center cut fillet of beef

Salt and fresh ground black pepper

1 tablespoon olive oil

FOR THE CHESTNUT CRUST

4 oz (115 g) chestnut purée

6 tablespoons soft salted butter

3 oz (85 g) Vermont cheddar cheese, grated

2 oz (50 g) roasted chestnuts, peeled

2 oz (50 g) fresh breadcrumbs

FOR THE PUMPKIN PANCAKE

4 oz (115 g) pumpkin purée

4 medium eggs

1 cup (8 fl. oz/250 ml) half and half cream

1 cup (8 fl. oz/250 ml) heavy cream

4 oz (115 g) all-purpose flour

FOR THE RED WINE SHALLOT SAUCE

½ cup (4 oz) shallots, fine diced

½ stick (4 tablespoons) unsalted butter

½ cup (4 fl. oz/100 ml) red wine (Cabernet Sauvignon)

2 teaspoons black peppercorns, crushed

2 cups (16 fl. oz/500 ml) veal jus

1 Start by making the chestnut crust. In a large bowl, mix all the crust ingredients together. Roll the resulting paste in greaseproof paper into a large tube. Reserve in a refrigerator ready to slice and use.

2 To make the pumpkin pancakes, combine all the pancake ingredients in a blender at high speed. Pour the mix into four buttered tart molds. Bake for 15 to 20 minutes in a 350 °F (175 °C) pre-heated oven.

3 Season the beef and roll in the olive oil. Broil the fillets of beef to the desired temperature.

4 In the meantime, make the red wine sauce. On a medium heat, sweat the shallots in the butter until translucent. Add the wine and crushed peppercorns. Reduce by half on a medium heat. Add the veal jus, boil, and reduce further until the sauce coats the back of a spoon. Season to taste.

5 Slice the chestnut crust and place a slice on top of each filet. Put under a broiler for a few minutes to glaze. Place a pancake on a plate with the glazed beef on top. Pour the shallot sauce around the beef. Serve with steamed carrots, cauliflower, or broccoli.

WINE Cabernet Sauvignon

CÔTES DE BŒUF SAUCE BÉARNAISE

Beef ribs with béarnaise sauce

A great classic of French bistro cuisine. The béarnaise sauce can be prepared in advance, and kept warm in a Thermos until you are ready to serve. Serve with matchstick fries.

SERVES 4 • 15 MINUTES PREPARATION • 1 HOUR COOKING

2 shallots

4 sprigs tarragon

8 sprigs chervil

¼ cup (1½ fl. oz/50 ml) dry white wine

¼ cup (1½ fl. oz/50 ml) wine vinegar

2 medium egg yolks

1 stick (8 tablespoons) salted butter

Salt and fresh ground black pepper

1 beef rib roast weighing 2 lb, 4 oz (1 kg)

Few sprigs chervil and tarragon, to garnish

1 Peel and chop the shallots. Strip the leaves off the tarragon and chervil sprigs and chop finely. Reserve the herbs.

2 Put the shallots, wine, and vinegar in a saucepan, and reduce by two thirds. Preheat the oven to 450 °F (230 °C).

3 Away from the heat, add 1 tablespoon cold water, then the egg yolks. Whisk together, and place over a very low heat to thicken. As soon as you can see the bottom of the saucepan while you are whisking, start adding the butter in small pieces, whisking continuously.

4 When all the butter has been added, add the chopped herbs and season with salt and pepper. The sauce can be kept warm by placing the pot in a pan of warm water, but should never be heated up rapidly or boiled.

5 Meanwhile, roast the beef in the oven for 20 minutes. Turn down the temperature to 425 °F (220 °C) and cook for another 40 minutes. Serve off the bone, in thick steaks, garnished with chervil and tarragon.

WINE Bordeaux

Côtes de bœuf sauce béarnaise

MEAT AND POULTRY

COQ AU VIN JAUNE

Chicken in vin jaune

A delicious recipe from the Jura, which calls for the choicest fowl and above all the use of vin jaune, a dry white wine from the Jura. If vin jaune is unavailable you can substitute it with dry sherry. For a slightly exotic touch, try adding a pinch of curry powder.

SERVES 6 TO 8 • 20 MINUTES PREPARATION • 45 MINUTES COOKING

3½ oz (100 g) dried morel mushrooms

1 large chicken, jointed into pieces

Juice of 1 lemon

6 tablespoons salted butter

1 scant cup (7 fl. oz/200 ml) vin jaune or dry white wine

1 scant cup (7 fl. oz/200 ml) crème fraîche

Pinch of curry powder, optional

Salt and fresh ground black pepper

Few sprigs of chervil, to garnish

1 Soak the mushrooms in a bowl of cold water.

2 Rub the chicken pieces with lemon juice.

3 Melt the butter in a casserole dish and brown the chicken pieces well on all sides.

4 Pour in the vin jaune, scraping the base of the casserole thoroughly with a wooden spoon to incorporate all the cooking juices. Continue cooking for 15 minutes over a gentle heat.

5 Add the drained morels, the crème fraîche, and the curry powder if using. Mix well, and allow to simmer for 10 minutes until the sauce thickens.

6 Season and serve, sprinkled with finely chopped chervil.

WINE A wine from the Jura (Arbois or vin jaune)

SAUTÉ DE VEAU

Veal with preserved lemons

Serve this with steamed zucchini, sprinkled with chopped fresh cilantro and drizzled with a little olive oil. Veal flank may be prepared in the same way.

SERVES 6 • 30 MINUTES PREPARATION • 5 MINUTES COOKING

2 large onions

3 salt-preserved lemons

2 tablespoons olive oil

2 lb, 4 oz (1 kg) shoulder of veal, cubed

⅔ cup (5 fl. oz/150 ml) veal or chicken broth

1 tablespoon coriander seeds

Salt and fresh ground black pepper

24 small black olives, pitted

1 Peel the onions and cut them into eight wedges. Cut the lemons into quarters and scrape away the flesh with a spoon so that only the rind remains.

2 Heat the olive oil in a cast-iron casserole dish on the stove and brown the veal cubes evenly, a few at a time. When they are all browned, return them to the casserole dish with the onions and the lemon rind pieces, turn down the heat, cover, and wait until the meat, onions, and lemons start to produce a liquid.

3 Pour in the broth, add the coriander seeds, and season. Cover again and allow to simmer gently for ¾ hour over a low heat.

4 About 10 minutes or so before the veal is cooked, add the pitted olives.

WINE A white wine from Languedoc-Roussillon

TOURNEDOS ROSSINI

Steak with foie gras and truffles

A real classic of great French cuisine. To impart a little more contrast to the recipe, arrange each steak on a slice of bread fried on both sides in a little butter.

SERVES 4 • 25 MINUTES PREPARATION • ABOUT 15 MINUTES COOKING

4 thin slices foie gras

All-purpose flour, for dusting

Salted butter, for frying

4 tournedos (small, round beefsteak cut from the tenderloin)

2 tablespoons Madeira

1 cup (8 fl. oz/250 ml) crème fraîche

Salt and fresh ground black pepper

1 truffle

1 Dust the foie gras lightly with flour and shake off the excess. Heat a little butter in a skillet and fry the foie gras for 3 minutes each side. Remove from the skillet and keep warm.

2 Cook the tournedos for a maximum of 5 minutes each side in the same skillet. Remove from the skillet and keep warm.

3 Discard the frying butter, return the skillet to a high heat, pour in the Madeira, and carefully ignite to flambé. When the flames have died down, add the crème fraîche and bring to a boil, scraping the base of the skillet thoroughly to incorporate all the cooking juices. Season.

4 Cut the truffle into thin slices.

5 Place the tournedos on individual plates, top with a slice of foie gras, and one or two slices of truffle, and cover with the sauce. Serve with creamy mashed potato.

WINE A red Burgundy (Pommard) or Bordeaux (Pomerol)

JARRETS DE PORC À LA BIÈRE

Pork hocks in beer

When cooking recipes from the Alsace region, spices are very important, and this recipe is rich in various flavors and aromas.

SERVES 6 • 30 MINUTES PREPARATION • 2 HOURS COOKING

6 pork hocks each weighing 1 to 1½ lb (450 to 700 g)

1 teaspoon paprika

1 teaspoon allspice

3 medium onions

1 bouquet garni (*see* Glossary, page 12)

3 medium cloves garlic

1 teaspoon ground cumin

4½ cups (36 fl. oz/1 l) light beer

1 Prick the skin of the pork hocks and roll them in the paprika mixed with the allspice.

2 Put the casserole on the stove, put in the hocks, and cover. After 8 minutes, turn the hocks, cover them again, and continue cooking them for a further 8 minutes.

3 After this time, pour two ladlefuls of water into the casserole.

4 Add the onions, the bouquet garni, and the garlic and the cumin which are minced together, and pour in 1 cup (8 fl. oz/250 ml) of the beer.

5 Put the casserole in the oven, preheated to 400 °F (200 °C) and cook, uncovered, for 2 hours, basting the hocks regularly with the remaining 3 cups (25 fl. oz/750 ml) of beer. Serve with a soft cheese such as cream cheese or cottage cheese, and herb quenelles (*see* page 87).

WINE A white Alsace wine (Riesling or Gewurztraminer)

ENTRECÔTE
SAUCE MARCHAND DE VIN

Broiled entrecôte steaks with red wine sauce

This is a modern reworking of a classic French recipe, in which the red wine sauce, known as sauce Marchand de vin, was thickened with a roux—a cooked mixture of melted butter and flour used to thicken sauces—though it still needs to be reduced for a long time. Use a fairly acidic red wine, such as a Beaujolais or Gamay.

SERVES 4 • 1 HOUR PREPARATION • 15 MINUTES COOKING

1 small carrot

1 small onion

1 celery stalk

1 medium tomato

2 shallots

5 tablespoons salted butter

1 sprig thyme

2¼ cups (17 fl. oz/500 ml) veal broth

1 cup (8 fl.oz/250 ml) red wine

2 entrecôte (boned rib) steaks, each weighing 12 oz to 14 oz (350 g to 400 g)

Salt and fresh ground black pepper

1 First, prepare the broth for the sauce: peel the carrot and the onion, trim the celery stalk, and chop them all coarsely. Chop the tomato. Peel the shallots, chop them, and set aside.

2 Melt 1 tablespoon butter in a saucepan and brown the chopped vegetables except the tomato. Add the thyme, tomato, and the veal broth and allow to simmer gently for 45 minutes. After this time, strain the vegetables and set aside, reserving the liquor. Boil the liquor to reduce it to a syrupy consistency.

3 Bring the red wine to a boil in a small saucepan and cook until reduced by half.

4 Broil the entrecôtes for 5 minutes each side then transfer to a plate, cover with another plate, and keep warm.

5 Melt 1 tablespoon butter in a small saucepan, add the shallots, the reduced wine, and the broth; when the mixture thickens, lower the heat and add the remaining butter, whisking it to bind the sauce.

6 Season, slice, and garnish the entrecôtes with chopped parsley. Pour the sauce over the entrecôtes, and serve with asparagus and baby carrots.

WINE Beaujolais

POULE FARÇIE

Stuffed chicken Périgord style

French tradition stipulates that the chicken be browned in goose fat. This is not strictly necessary, although it does give the chicken some color and, of course, a little extra flavor.

SERVES 6 • 30 MINUTES PREPARATION • 2½ HOURS COOKING

1 chicken weighing about 4 lb (1.8 kg), liver reserved

FOR THE STUFFING

2 slices country bread

1 cup (8 fl. oz/250 ml) milk

2 medium cloves garlic

½ small bunch flat-leaf parsley

½ small bunch chervil

½ small bunch chives

3½ oz (100 g) salt pork

The reserved chicken liver

2 medium egg yolks

Salt and fresh ground black pepper

FOR THE VEGETABLES

5 medium carrots

1 turnip

1 large leek

2 celery stalks

2 medium potatoes

2 oz (50 g) goose fat

1 large onion

2 cloves

FOR THE SAUCE

½ small bunch flat-leaf parsley

½ small bunch chervil

½ small bunch chives

2 shallots

1 medium egg

⅔ cup (5 fl. oz/150 ml) walnut oil

1 tablespoon wine vinegar

TO SERVE

Gherkins

Coarse sea salt

Country bread, toasted and rubbed with garlic

1 First, make the stuffing. Cut off the crusts from the slices of bread and discard. Soak the bread in the milk. Peel and mince the garlic cloves. Wash and chop the parsley, chervil, and chives. Finely chop the salt pork and break up the bread. Clean out the chicken and reserve the liver. Mix all the above ingredients in a bowl, together with the liver from the chicken, crushed with a fork. Bind with two egg yolks. Season, then stuff the chicken cavity with the mixture. Sew up the opening with kitchen string and truss the chicken, taking care not to mark the skin.

2 Wash and peel the carrots, turnips, leeks, celery, and potatoes, and cut them up if they are too large.

3 In a large stockpot, brown the chicken on all sides in the goose fat for 5 minutes. Discard the fat and cover the chicken with boiling water. Add the onion pricked with the cloves and the prepared vegetables separated from the potatoes. Season, and bring to a boil. Carefully skim the broth, reduce the heat to a minimum, and cook, covered, for 2 hours.

4 Add the potatoes and cook for 20 minutes more.

5 Make the sauce. Wash and chop the parsley, chervil, and chives. Peel and finely slice the shallots. Hard-cook the egg for 10 minutes in the broth and remove its shell. Combine the walnut oil, vinegar, herbs, shallots, the finely chopped hard-cooked egg, and salt and pepper. Beat well to emulsify the sauce and set aside.

6 Transfer the chicken to a serving dish and surround with the vegetables, a few gherkins, and a bowl of coarse sea salt. Serve the sauce separately and pour the strained broth over slices of toasted country bread rubbed with garlic.

WINE A Bordeaux or a red from southwest France (Cahors or Madiran)

PORC AUX CHAMPIGNONS

Pork with mushrooms

The art of simmering is a very important part of bistro cooking: all you have to do is combine all the ingredients, put them in the casserole dish, and allow to cook before enjoying the rich flavors.

SERVES 4 • 25 MINUTES PREPARATION • 1 HOUR COOKING

2 pork tenderloins, each weighing 14 oz (400 g)

Olive oil, for frying

Salt and fresh ground black pepper

1 lb, 2 oz (500 g) button mushrooms

1 bay leaf

2 cloves

3 shallots

8 baby onions

1 small sprig thyme

1 cup (8 fl. oz/250 ml) light cream

1 Cut the pork tenderloins into large pieces.

2 Heat a little olive oil in a skillet and brown the meat on all sides. Season.

3 Wipe the mushrooms, slice them thinly, and add to the skillet with the bay leaf and cloves.

4 Peel the shallots and baby onions. Slice the shallots and add them to the skillet with the whole onions and the sprig of thyme.

5 Cover and cook for 1 hour over a gentle heat.

6 Add the cream and bring to a boil, stirring constantly so the sauce thickens. Season to taste and serve with fresh boiled rice.

WINE A white Burgundy (Rully or Pouilly-Fuissé)

NAVARIN D'AGNEAU PRINTANIER

Navarin of spring lamb

It is important to select a casserole dish just large enough to hold the lamb pieces in a single layer without their being too crowded. It is also important to take out the meat, decant the cooking juices, and rinse the casserole dish to remove any splinters of bone before cooking the final 45 minutes. It is essential to cook this casserole over a low heat. If preferred, cook it in the oven at 350 °F (180 °C).

SERVES 4 • 30 MINUTES PREPARATION • 1½ HOURS COOKING

4 medium tomatoes

6 small carrots

6 small new turnips

8 small onions

8 small new potatoes

14 oz (400 g) baby peas (petits pois), in the pod

½ stick (4 tablespoons) salted butter

14 oz (400 g) lamb chops, in pieces

10½ oz (300 g) shoulder of lamb, in pieces

Salt and fresh ground black pepper

1 level tablespoon all-purpose flour

1 medium clove garlic

1 bouquet garni (*see* **Glossary**, page 12)

1 Peel the tomatoes then seed and chop them. Wash the other vegetables and peel. Cut into lengths or into quarters. Shell the peas.

2 Melt the butter in a cast-iron casserole dish over a moderate heat and brown the meat pieces (chops and shoulder of lamb). Stir them around well so that they brown on all sides. Season. When they are golden-brown, sprinkle in a little flour and stir again. Add the tomatoes, the whole peeled garlic clove, and the bouquet garni. Top up with water.

3 Simmer over gentle heat for 45 minutes, then remove the meat pieces with a slotted spoon and put the juices through a strainer.

4 Return the meat and juices to the rinsed, dried casserole and bring back to a boil. Then add all the vegetables except the peas.

5 Cook for 30 minutes over a gentle heat. Add the peas and cook for a further 15 minutes.

WINE A red Burgundy (Volnay)

RISOTTO AUX ŒUFS DE CANNE

Duck egg and white truffle risotto with Brie and young leeks

This recipe comes from a traditional French bistro in the Yarra Valley, Australia. The combination of the duck eggs and white truffles is truly wonderful. The brie adds to the creamy, rich texture, and the leeks add a touch of color.

SERVES 6 • 30 MINUTES PREPARATION • 45 MINUTES COOKING

1 medium onion, diced

3 tablespoons fresh thyme, chopped

2 medium cloves garlic, sliced

2 tablespoons olive oil

2¼ cups (1lb, 2 oz/500 g) arborio risotto rice

¾ cup (6 fl. oz/150 ml) white wine

4 cups (32 fl. oz/1 l) hot chicken broth

3 duck eggs

7 oz (200 g) cream Brie

1 young leek

1 oz (30 g) white truffle, grated

Salt and fresh ground black pepper

1 In a saucepan, sweat the onion, thyme, and garlic in olive oil.

2 When soft, add the rice, and mix in thoroughly until it is coated in olive oil. Deglaze with the white wine and cook for about 10 minutes until almost dry.

3 Over a medium heat, add in three parts of the hot chicken broth, stirring continuously in between each addition.

4 In the meantime, put the duck eggs in boiling water for 4 to 5 minutes, then place under cold running water and peel.

5 Roughly chop the brie and slice the leek finely. Grate the white truffle.

6 Take 10½ oz (300 g) of cooked hot rice and fork through the leeks until soft. Then add the Brie until melted. Roughly crush the eggs in the risotto and mix thoroughly. Add the truffles, season with salt and pepper.

WINE Sauvignon Blanc

CARBONADE

Carbonade of beef

A specialty from northern France, where they like to introduce sweet flavors to savory dishes. To add a little spice to the dish, some chefs recommend spreading a little mustard on the slices of gingerbread.

SERVES 6 • 40 MINUTES PREPARATION • 3 HOURS COOKING

3 lb, 5 oz (1.5 kg) beef, preferably chuck steak

Salt and fresh ground black pepper

½ cup (100 g) lard

3 tablespoons all-purpose flour

10½ oz (300 g) onions

3 tablespoons wine vinegar

4 cups (36 fl. oz/1 l) light beer

3 tablespoons soft brown sugar

4 slices gingerbread

1 bay leaf

1 sprig thyme

2 cloves

1 Cut the meat into 12 even-size portions and season.

2 Heat the lard in a cast-iron casserole dish and brown the beef pieces for 4 minutes each side. Add the flour and the finley chopped onions and allow to cook for 5 minutes.

3 Pour in the vinegar while scraping the bottom of the casserole thoroughly with a wooden spoon to incorporate all the cooking juices. Pour in the beer.

4 Add the sugar, gingerbread, bay leaf, thyme, and cloves. Season, cover, and allow to simmer over a very low heat for 3 hours.

WINE A red from the Languedoc-Roussillon (Corbières or Saint-Chignan)

4 ACCOMPANIMENTS

RAGOÛT DE LÉGUMES NOUVEAUX

Ragout of new vegetables

The vegetables should be crisp but cooked. Make sure you remove the tough outer leaves from the artichokes—it is better to remove an extra layer of leaves to make sure the rest is tender. A dash of a very fruity olive oil may be added at the end.

SERVES 6 • 1 HOUR PREPARATION • 25 MINUTES COOKING

2 lb, 4 oz (1 kg) fava beans

1 lb, 2 oz (500 g) fresh peas, in the pod

12 medium artichokes

1 lemon

1 lb, 2 oz (500 g) green asparagus

1 bunch scallions

1 thick slice cooked ham

⅔ cup (5 fl. oz/150 ml) olive oil

½ cup (4 fl. oz/100 ml) chicken broth

Pinch of dried oregano or fresh marjoram

Salt and fresh ground black pepper

1 Shell and remove the skin from the fava beans; set aside. Shell the peas and set aside. Prepare the artichokes: break off the stalks, remove the tough leaves from the outside, cutting off the sharp ends of the leaves with scissors and, turning the base, cutting them in half (or into quarters if they are large) lengthwise. Remove and discard the hairy choke. Rub each artichoke section with a half lemon and put them in water with a dash of lemon juice to prevent discoloration. Set aside. Cut the asparagus into 2-inch (5-cm) pieces, keeping the tips separately to one side. Clean the scallions and cut the stalks to 2 inches (5 cm). Set aside.

2 Cut the ham into ^{5}⁄$_8$- x 2-inch (1.5- x 5-cm) rectangles.

3 Gently heat the olive oil in a cast-iron casserole dish and brown the ham, the half artichokes, and the scallions. Stir well, moisten with a little chicken broth, and cover. Allow to cook for 5 to 6 minutes.

4 Add the peas, the asparagus except for the tips, and a generous pinch of oregano or marjoram. Stir gently and allow to cook for a further 5 minutes.

5 Add the asparagus tips, without stirring, and cook for another 5 minutes.

6 Finally, add the beans, still without mixing, and cook for a further 5 minutes.

7 Make sure that there is still enough liquid in the pot and add a little broth after the addition of each vegetable if necessary. Cover the pot after each addition.

8 Season with a little salt and pepper.

FRITES DE POTIMARRON

Pumpkin fries

The pleasant, sweet flavor of pumpkin lends itself well to this way of cooking. This makes a good accompaniment to the Thanksgiving turkey, and any Christmas poultry.

SERVES 4 • 15 MINUTES PREPARATION • 20 MINUTES COOKING

One 2¾ lb (1.2 kg) fresh pumpkin

Vegetable oil, for deep-frying

Celery salt

1 celery leaf, to garnish

1 Remove the pumpkin skin and scoop out the seeds. Cut the flesh lengthwise into thick slices, then cut into "fries."

2 Wrap the fries in a dish towel and dry them carefully, taking care because they are fragile and can break. Leave them wrapped in the dish towel for 15 minutes.

3 In a heavy-based, high-sided skillet suitable for deep-frying, heat sufficient vegetable oil in which to fry the pumpkin fries to 350 °F (180°C).

4 Cook the fries in batches. Place a small quantity of fries in a frying basket and deep-fry for 3 minutes, until golden-brown and crisp. Drain the basket and empty the fries carefully onto a tray lined with paper towels. Repeat until all the pumpkin fries are done, allowing the oil to heat up again between cooking one batch of fries and the next.

5 Sprinkle the drained fries with celery salt and keep warm until they are all cooked.

6 Garnish with a celery leaf.

Frites de potimarron

QUENELLES AU FROMAGE BLANC

Soft cheese and herb quenelles

A recipe from Alsace, these delicate dumplings are not complicated to make, as long as you check the dough's consistency before you cook them and, if necessary, add a little more flour for added firmness.

SERVES 6 • 30 MINUTES PREPARATION • 10 MINUTES COOKING

2 lb, 4 oz (1 kg) cream cheese

6 large eggs

4 cups (1lb, 2oz/500 g) all-purpose flour

Salt and fresh ground black pepper

Pinch of freshly grated nutmeg

1 teaspoon chopped parsley

1 teaspoon chopped chives

1 Mix the cream cheese with the eggs and flour. Season and add a little grated nutmeg, chopped parsley, and chives.

2 Mix well to form a uniform dough.

3 Bring some salted water to a boil in a large saucepan.

4 Test the dough by taking a small amount in a teaspoon and placing it into the boiling water: if the dough falls apart, add a little more flour.

5 Take spoonfuls of the dough and, using two teaspoons, shape into oval dumplings. Carefully lower a few quenelles into the water and poach for 10 minutes.

6 Drain and keep warm in a hot oven while you poach the remaining quenelles.

NAVETS FARÇIS AUX LÉGUMES ET À LA CARDAMONE

Stuffed turnips with cardamom

A good accompaniment to white meats and a flavorful way of using up winter turnips before the new ones appear in spring.

SERVES 4 • 20 MINUTES PREPARATION • 35 MINUTES COOKING

4 oz (100 g) button mushrooms

2 shallots

1 celery stalk

2 medium slices cooked ham

12 medium turnips

1 stick (8 tablespoons) salted butter

Salt and pepper

Seeds from 5 white cardamom pods

Few sprigs chervil, to garnish

1 Wash the mushrooms and cut off the stems. Peel the shallots and chop them finely. Trim the celery and dice very small. Cut the slices of ham into very thin julienne strips.

2 Peel the turnips and hollow out, leaving a thickness of $^1\!/_2$-inch (1-cm). Bring some salted water to a boil in a large saucepan and blanch the turnips for 3 minutes. Drain and refresh in cold water.

3 Melt 2 tablespoons of butter in a high-sided skillet. Cook the mushrooms and shallots in the butter for 3 minutes over a low heat without allowing them to brown. Add the ham and the celery, followed by the seasoning and cardamom seeds, and cook for 5 minutes.

4 Preheat the oven to 350 °F (180 °C).

5 Using a small spoon, stuff the turnips with the mixture in the saucepan. With the remaining butter, thoroughly grease a baking dish, just big enough to hold the turnips. Arrange the stuffed turnips in the dish. Pour in cold water to three-quarters to cover the turnips and cover with foil. Bake for 30 minutes or until the turnips are tender. Keep them warm in their serving dish.

6 Transfer the cooking liquor to a saucepan. Reduce over a high heat until it coats a spoon and pour over the turnips. Sprinkle with the chervil and serve very hot.

ACCOMPANIMENTS

PATRANQUE

Bread and bacon pancake

If liked, add a finely chopped clove of garlic at the same time as the bread. This dish goes very well with sausages.

SERVES 4 • 15 MINUTES PREPARATION • 30 MINUTES COOKING

1 lb, 2 oz (500 g) stale brown bread or sourdough bread

3 oz (85 g) bacon slices

1 medium clove of garlic, chopped fine, optional

9 oz (250 g) Tomme de Cantal cheese or mozzarella

1 Remove the crusts from the bread and crumble coarsely. If the bread is very stale it may be softened with a little water.

2 Cut the bacon into very small pieces. Slice the cheese thinly.

3 Cook the bacon pieces in a skillet over a moderate heat until they are completely transparent and begin to crisp.

4 Add the bread to the bacon in the skillet and stir it about so that it soaks up the fat from the bacon and starts to break up. Add the garlic if using. When it begins to brown, add the slices of cheese and stir well, then reduce the heat. Add salt and plenty of pepper.

5 Allow to brown for about 10 minutes.

6 When a crust has formed, remove the pancake and turn it over, using a spatula and a plate, so that the other side can brown for 5 to 10 minutes.

7 Slide it into a dish and serve with a slightly bitter-flavored green salad, dressed with walnut oil.

CŒURS DE CÉLERI BRAISÉS

Braised celery hearts

If your celery is on the large side, break off the stalks, remove the strings with a vegetable peeler and cut them into 2 to 2½-inch (5 to 6-cm) lengths.

SERVES 4 • 10 MINUTES PREPARATION • 45 MINUTES COOKING

1 small carrot

1 small onion

5 or 6 celery hearts

½ stick (4 tablespoons) salted butter

Salt and fresh ground black pepper

2½ cups (17 fl. oz/500 ml) veal or chicken broth

1 bouquet garni (*see* Glossary, page 12)

1 Peel the carrot and onion, and chop and dice them into small pieces.

2 Remove the outer stalks of the celery to reveal the hearts. Keep them whole, removing just the leaves and the woody parts.

3 Rinse the celery hearts and blanch them for 5 minutes in well-salted boiling water. Drain and cool immediately in cold water.

4 Preheat the oven to 350 °F (180 °C).

5 Melt the butter in a heavy casserole over low heat. Add the carrot and onion and fry them gently, without browning, until they are soft.

6 Add the well-drained celery, season, and cover with the broth. Add the bouquet garni, cover, and place in the oven. After 20 minutes, take out the casserole, turn over the celery that is not immersed in liquid, and return to the oven for a further 20 minutes. Serve with a white fish.

GRATIN DE MACARONIS

Macaroni cheese

A classic bistro dish from the city of Lyons, where they never hesitate to add an extra bit of cream! This recipe is interesting in its use of two cheeses, each one contributing its own distinct flavor.

SERVES 6 • 20 MINUTES PREPARATION • 25 TO 30 MINUTES COOKING

1 lb, 2 oz (500 g) macaroni

¼ stick (25 g) salted butter

¼ cup (25 g) all-purpose flour

2¼ cups (17 fl. oz/500 ml) crème fraîche

Salt and fresh ground black pepper

1 teaspoon grated nutmeg

3½ oz (100 g) **Comté, Emmenthal, or Gruyère cheese**, grated

½ cup (2 oz/50 g) grated **Parmesan cheese**

1 Preheat the oven to 400 °F (200 °C). Add the macaroni to a large pan of boiling salted water. Allow to cook until the pasta is still a little firm and drain.

2 Melt the butter in a saucepan over a low heat. Add the flour while whisking steadily. Add the crème fraîche and seasonings and, finally, the nutmeg and the grated Comté, Emmenthal, or Gruyère cheese.

3 Put the macaroni in a gratin dish. Pour the sauce over it and top with the grated Parmesan cheese.

4 Bake in the oven for 25 to 30 minutes, until golden-brown.

Gratin de macaronis

PETITS POIS À LA FRANÇAISE

Peas with scallions and lettuce

The sugar enhances the sweetness of the peas, which is further accentuated by the bitterness of the salad. A few small pieces of cooked ham may also be added at the beginning.

SERVES 4 • 30 MINUTES PREPARATION • 15 MINUTES COOKING

3 lb, 5 oz (1.5 kg) baby peas (petits pois), in the pod

12 scallions

2 small lettuce hearts, halved

6 tablespoons salted butter

Salt

Pinch of sugar

½ cup (4 fl. oz/100 ml) chicken broth

Few sprigs chervil, to garnish

1 Shell the peas, clean the scallions, rinse the lettuces and cut them vertically into half.

2 Melt half the butter in a skillet and fry the scallions gently without allowing them to brown. Add the halved lettuce hearts and then the peas. Season with a little salt and a pinch of sugar. Add the broth, cover, and cook for 10 to 15 minutes.

3 When the peas are done, add the remaining butter in pieces, stir well, and transfer to a serving dish while still very hot. Sprinkle with sprigs of chervil, to garnish.

POMMES DE TERRE
AU REBLOCHON

Baked potatoes with Reblochon cheese

These baked potatoes, topped with melted cheese and chopped bacon, are a perfect accompaniment to white meats. They can also be served on their own as a main dish, along with a little charcuterie (cold cuts of meat) and a green salad. If Reblochon is unavailable, substitute with another soft cheese that is easy to melt, like Brie or Monterey Jack.

**SERVES 4 • 20 MINUTES PREPARATION •
ABOUT 1 HOUR COOKING**

½ **Reblochon cheese, or 4 oz (125 g)
Brie, or Monterey Jack**

4 thin slices bacon

4 large baking potatoes

Olive oil, for brushing

½ **stick (4 tablespoons) salted butter**

1 Cut the cheese, with its rind, into pieces. Chop the bacon and fry in a little oil or broil.

2 Scrub clean and dry the potatoes. Brush them with a little olive oil and cook them in the oven for 1 hour at 425 °F (220 °C), being sure to turn them halfway through.

3 Remove the baked potatoes from the oven and cut in half lengthwise. Carefully scoop out three quarters of each potato from its skin.

4 Preheat the oven broiler. Place a large piece of butter in each half potato then place them under the broiler for 10 minutes until they are golden-brown.

5 Remove from the broiler and stuff each half potato with a little cheese, followed by some chopped bacon and scooped-out potato flesh.

6 Put back under the broiler for a few minutes, then serve immediately.

Pommes de terre au reblochon

Onion marmalade

Similar to chutney, this onion marmalade can be served hot, sprinkled with cumin seed, alongside meat or game, or cold, as a condiment to a terrine.

MAKES 2 LB, 4 OZ (1 KG) • 25 MINUTES PREPARATION • 45 MINUTES COOKING

2 lb, 4 oz (1 kg) yellow onions

½ stick (4 tablespoons) salted butter

¼ cup (2 oz/50 g) raisins

½ cup (4 fl. oz/100 ml) grenadine syrup

½ cup (4 fl. oz/100 ml) wine vinegar

Salt and fresh ground black pepper

Pinch of ground ginger

1 teaspoon cumin seeds

1 Peel the onions and chop them finely, preferably using a food processor. Heat the butter in a skillet, add the onions, and soften them gently, stirring constantly to stop them browning, for about 10 minutes.

2 Next add the raisins, grenadine syrup, and vinegar. Add the seasoning and ginger, mix thoroughly, and cover the skillet. Reduce the heat to a minimum, then allow the ingredients to blend together gently, stirring from time to time, until the cooking liquid has evaporated and the onions are well reduced. This should take about 45 minutes. Sprinkle the onion marmalade with cumin seeds if serving hot.

GRATIN DE POMMES DE TERRE SAVOYARD

Potato gratin

A simple recipe that is especially delicious if made with the broth left over from a chicken casserole or pot au feu. If none is available, make your own broth by boiling some chicken or guinea fowl wings in enough water for at least 1 hour with one carrot, one celery stalk, one leek, one onion, a bouquet garni (see Glossary, page 12), and a little salt and pepper.

SERVES 6 • 20 MINUTES PREPARATION • 1 HOUR COOKING

1 medium clove garlic, peeled

2 lb, 4 oz (1 kg) medium potatoes

Salt

2¼ cups (17 fl. oz/500 ml) chicken or other broth

2 tablespoons salted butter

1 Preheat the oven to 375 °F (190 °C). Rub a gratin dish with garlic.

2 Peel and wash the potatoes. Cut them into thin slices.

3 Arrange the slices in a gratin dish, adding a little salt between the layers. Cover with broth.

4 Bring to a boil on the stove, cover with a sheet of foil, and cook in the oven for 1 hour.

5 Remove from the oven, take off the foil, and dot thickly with butter.

6 Return to the oven for a few minutes until the top is golden-brown and serve immediately.

WINE A white wine from Savoy (Apremont)

CAROTTES VICHY

Carrots Vichy

A great classic, these glazed carrots are always delicious when new carrots are in season. For a slightly exotic touch, add a little ground cumin just before serving. The water and sugar may be replaced with orange juice.

SERVES 4 • 20 MINUTES PREPARATION • 30 MINUTES COOKING

2 lb, 4oz (1 kg) new carrots

½ stick (4 tablespoons) salted butter

1 teaspoon sugar

Salt and fresh ground black pepper

1 small bunch parsley

1 Peel the carrots and cut into thin round slices. Put them into a heavy skillet with the butter, sugar, and a generous pinch of salt.

2 Cover with cold water and bring quickly to a boil, then lower the heat.

3 Cook, uncovered, over a gentle heat until all the water has been absorbed and the carrots are bathed in the butter and sugar.

4 Keep a careful eye on the carrots and do not allow them to brown once the water has evaporated.

5 Wash and dry the parsley and chop it finely. Turn the carrots into a dish and sprinkle with parsley before serving.

POMMES DE TERRE FARÇIES
À LA BERRICHONNE

Stuffed potatoes à la berrichonne

If preferred, you can replace the bacon with some cooked ham. This is quite a nourishing dish, which can be served as a meal in its own right accompanied by a green salad or a little charcuterie (cold cuts of meat).

SERVES 6 • 20 MINUTES PREPARATION • 40 MINUTES COOKING

6 large baking potatoes

2 small onions

5½ oz (150 g) bacon slices

½ stick (4 tablespoons) salted butter

1 sprig thyme

Salt and fresh ground black pepper

5½ oz (150 g) button mushrooms

½ cup (4 fl. oz/100 ml) crème fraîche

1¾ oz (50 g) Saint-Nectaire cheese or Brie, rind removed, and diced

1 Preheat the oven to 400 °F (200 °C). Wash the potatoes and wrap each one in foil. Place the foil-wrapped potatoes on a baking tray in the center of the oven and cook for 35 minutes.

2 Meanwhile, peel and chop the onions. Dice the bacon. Brown the onions and bacon in a skillet in 2 tablespoons butter. Add the thyme, salt (depending on how salty the bacon is), and pepper.

3 Peel the mushrooms, slice thinly, and braise in a covered saucepan with the remaining butter.

4 Drain the contents of the skillet and the saucepan and mix together.

5 When the potatoes are done (test with the point of a knife), remove from the oven and take off the foil. Slice off a lid lengthwise from each one and hollow them out carefully with a spoon. Mash the potatos in a bowl, blending in the crème fraîche, then add the cooked mushroom, onion mixture, and the diced cheese. Adjust the seasoning.

6 Stuff the potatoes with this mixture. Place them on a baking tray and reheat in a hot oven for 5 minutes. Serve immediately.

5 DESSERTS

FIGUES POCHÉES
À LA CANNELLE

Poached figs with cinnamon

A delicious dessert to be served well-chilled, with homemade shortbread cookies or vanilla ice cream.

SERVES 8 • 20 MINUTES COOKING • 15 MINUTES PREPARATION

2¼ cups (17 fl. oz/500 ml) water

¾ cup (5½ oz/150 g) superfine sugar

1 vanilla bean

1 teaspoon ground cinnamon

4 tablespoons dark rum

16 purple figs

1 Put the water and sugar in a skillet. Bring to just below boiling point over a medium heat. As soon as the sugar has completely dissolved to a syrupy consistency, remove from the heat.

2 Split the vanilla bean in two and scrape the inside, and add to the syrup in the skillet.

3 In a small bowl, mix the cinnamon with the rum, then pour into the skillet. Stir well and allow to cool to lukewarm temperature.

4 Wash and dry the figs. Score them lightly in a criss-cross shape on the rounded part, without cutting too deeply into the flesh.

5 Bring the syrup back to a simmering point and carefully lower in the figs.

6 Remove immediately from the heat and allow the figs to cool in the syrup.

7 To serve, remove the vanilla bean from the syrup, arrange the figs in a shallow dish, and cover them with the syrup.

WINE Banyuls

GÂTEAU GLACÉ AU CITRON

Frosted lemon cake

The lemons may be replaced with oranges or mandarin oranges. A little finely diced candied orange, lemon, or grapefruit peel may also be added to the cake batter.

SERVES 6 • 30 MINUTES PREPARATION • 40 MINUTES COOKING

4 medium eggs, separated

1 cup (7 oz/200 g) superfine sugar

Rind and juice of 2 lemons

1⅔ cups (7 oz/200 g) all-purpose flour

Pinch of salt

2 teaspoons baking powder

2 sticks unsalted butter

FOR THE FROSTING

1½ cups (7 oz/200 g) confectioner's sugar

Candied lemon slices, to decorate

1 In a bowl, beat the egg yolks with the superfine sugar until the mixture leaves a trail for a few seconds when the whisk is lifted.

2 Wash and brush the lemons. Dry them and finely grate the rind. Stir into the egg and sugar mixture. Squeeze the juice from the lemons and add half to the mixture (reserve the other half for the frosting).

3 Mix together the flour, salt, and baking powder, then sift and add to the mixture.

4 Melt the butter over a low heat, then add it to the mixture.

5 Preheat the oven to 400 °F (200 °C).

6 Beat the egg whites until stiff. Fold gently into the mixture.

7 Line a 9-inch (22-cm) springform round cake pan with a sheet of baking paper, then pour in the mixture.

8 Bake in the center of the oven for 20 minutes, then score the top of the cake lengthwise with the blade of a knife. Continue baking for a further 20 minutes until rich, golden-brown, and firm to the touch.

9 Remove the cake from the oven, and turn it onto a rack. Remove the baking paper and allow the cake to cool completely.

10 When the cake is cool, make the frosting. Mix the confectioner's sugar with the reserved lemon juice. When it attains a thin, creamy consistency, use it to coat the cake evenly.

11 Allow to set before serving. Decorate with candied lemon slices.

WINE Muscat

PALETS FOURRÉS AU CHOCOLAT

Chocolate cookies with ganache filling

Melt the chocolate in a double boiler, or a heatproof bowl set over a saucepan of hot but not simmering water. Take care that not a single drop of water becomes mixed with the chocolate. The other possibility is to melt the chocolate in a microwave oven, providing you keep a close eye on it. Ganache is a mixture of cream and chocolate which is used as a frosting or filling for cakes and cookies.

MAKES 20 PALETS • 20 MINUTES PREPARATION (BEGIN THE GANACHE 1 HOUR IN ADVANCE) • 10 TO 12 MINUTES COOKING

FOR THE GANACHE

3½ oz (100 g) semisweet chocolate

¼ cup (2 fl. oz/60 ml) crème fraîche

2 tablespoons unsalted butter

FOR THE COOKIES

1½ sticks unsalted butter

½ cup (4 oz/125 g) sugar

2 medium eggs

1¼ cups (5½ oz/150 g) all-purpose flour

Unsweetened cocoa, for dusting

1 One hour before you plan to make the cookies, make the ganache for the filling. Melt the chocolate in a double boiler. Add the crème fraîche and butter little by little until you have a fairly soft chocolate cream, which will set when it cools.

2 Cream the butter and sugar in a bowl. Mix well. Add the eggs one by one, stirring continuously. The sugar must dissolve completely. Sprinkle on the flour and beat the mixture with a whisk.

3 Preheat the oven to 375 °F (190 °C). Butter a cookie sheet and dust it with flour. Using a tablespoon, place little heaps of the mixture, spaced well apart, on the sheet.

4 Bake for 10 to 12 minutes, then carefully transfer the cookies to a rack and allow to cool.

5 Turn the cookies upside down and spread with a little of the not-quite-set chocolate ganache. Sandwich the cookies together in pairs and dust with a little unsweetened cocoa.

WINE Banyuls or Port

STREUSSEL AUX POMMES

Apple streusel

Streussel, from the Alsace region, is quite similar to an English crumble. For a more sophisticated dessert, serve with vanilla ice cream, custard, a little Chantilly cream (whipped cream flavored with sugar and vanilla), or Cognac.

SERVES 8 • 30 MINUTES PREPARATION • 45 MINUTES COOKING

Unsalted butter, for greasing

¾ cup (5½ oz/150 g) sugar

¾ cup (2oz/50 g) currants

½ cup (2 oz/50 g) chopped mixed nuts

½ cup (2 oz/50 g) slivered almonds

1 tablespoon honey

6 tablespoons unsalted butter

1 tablespoon ground cinnamon

¾ cup (3½ oz/100 g) all-purpose flour

4½ lb (2 kg) cooking apples, chopped

Crème fraîche, to serve

1 Preheat the oven to 350 °F (180 °C). Grease a 9-inch (22-cm) round baking dish.

2 Mix ¼ cup (2 oz/50 g) sugar with the currants, chopped nuts, slivered almonds, and honey. Work the butter into the mixture, then add the remaining sugar, the cinnamon, and the flour. Using your fingertips, sprinkle this topping all over the apples.

3 Place in the oven and bake for 45 minutes. Serve with a dollop of crème fraîche.

WINE Choice of fine Alsace wines

CRÈME BRÛLÉE À LA CHICORÉE

Chicory cream desserts

Instead of the chicory-flavored coffee you can flavor the cream with unsweetened cocoa, ground almonds or hazelnuts, a pinch of spice (pepper or ginger, which goes particularly well with the unsweetened cocoa), or a few drops of Grand Marnier, Cointreau, or whiskey.

SERVES 4 • 20 MINUTES PREPARATION • 45 MINUTES COOKING

2¼ cups (17 fl. oz/500 ml) crème fraîche

3 teaspoons chicory-flavored finely-ground coffee

7 medium eggs

1 cup (5½ oz/150 g) soft light brown sugar

1 Preheat the oven to 325 °F (160 °C).

2 Bring the cream and coffee to a boil in a saucepan. As soon as it starts to boil, remove from the heat, cover, and allow to sit for 30 minutes.

3 Add the eggs and sugar to the saucepan. Mix together and turn into individual 4-inch (10-cm) round gratin dishes.

4 Place the dishes in a roasting pan half-filled with water, and cook for 45 minutes.

WINE Banyuls

CLAFOUTIS AUX CERISES

Cherries baked in batter

From Burgundy comes a version of this famous dessert, where it is known as "tartouillat." Slightly sharp, sour, unpitted cherries work best in this dessert.

SERVES 6 • 20 MINUTES PREPARATION • 25 MINUTES COOKING

2¼ cups (9 oz/250 g) all-purpose flour

Pinch of salt

½ cup (3½ oz/100 g) sugar

1 envelope vanilla sugar

4 medium eggs

¼ cup (1½ fl. oz/50 ml) dark rum

Scant 1 cup (7 fl. oz/200 ml) whole milk

1 stick (8 tablespoons) unsalted butter

3½ cups (1 lb, 10oz/750 g) ripe, unpitted cherries

1 Preheat the oven to 400 °F (200 °C).

2 Blend the flour, salt, sugar, and the vanilla sugar in a bowl. Make a well and add the eggs one at a time, then the rum and milk. Mix together.

3 Butter a deep 9 x 9-inch (22 x 22-cm) baking pan. Place the unpitted cherries and a few pieces of butter in the pan. Cover with the batter and bake for 25 minutes until the batter has set and the cherries have risen to the top.

WINE Banyuls

GÂTEAU BASQUE

Basque cake

*There are two versions of Basque cake, one based on cherry
preserves, the other on pastry cream (crème pâtissière).
We have chosen the latter which, whatever the season,
is always very popular.*

SERVES 8 • 50 MINUTES PREPARATION • 45 MINUTES COOKING

FOR THE DOUGH

½ cup (3½ oz/100 g) sugar

½ stick (4 tablespoons) unsalted butter, softened

¾ cup (3½ oz/100 g) all-purpose flour

⅛ oz (5 g) yeast

Pinch of salt

1 teaspoon rum

½ teaspoon vanilla extract

1 teaspoon almond extract

FOR THE PASTRY CREAM

1 cup (8 fl. oz/250 ml) milk

½ vanilla bean

2¼ cups (9oz/250 g) flour

⅜ cup (2½ oz/75 g) sugar

1 teaspoon rum

2 medium egg yolks

1 medium egg yolk, beaten, for the glaze

Confectioner's sugar, for dusting

Red currants, to decorate

1 To make the dough, combine all the dough ingredients
in a large bowl. Do not knead the resulting dough too
much. Allow it to rise for 2 to 3 hours.

2 To make the pastry cream, heat the milk in a saucepan
together with the vanilla bean split in half lengthwise.
Remove from the heat, cover, and allow the vanilla
to infuse for 20 minutes.

3 In a mixing bowl, combine the flour, sugar, rum, and
egg yolks. Remove the vanilla bean from the saucepan and
bring the milk back to a boil. Pour it over the flour and
sugar mixture. Mix all the ingredients together and
heat to boiling point.

4 Preheat the oven to 350 °F (180 °C).

5 Roll out two thirds of the dough to fit the base and
sides of a shallow 9-inch (22-cm) round cake pan. Spread
the filling over the dough and fold over the edges of the
dough. Brush the edge with a little beaten egg yolk, then roll
out the remaining dough to cover the filling completely.
Glaze with beaten egg yolk and bake for 45 minutes in a
preheated oven. Serve cold, dusted with confectioner's
sugar, and decorate with red currants.

WINE Jurançon

DESSERTS

POIRES AU VIN

Pears in wine

A dessert for autumn or winter, when new wine and pears come onto the market. The choice of spices and herbs is a matter of taste—some will add a little ground ginger or a few cardamom seeds, others might use honey instead of sugar, or prefer to omit the crème de cassis.

SERVES 6 • 15 MINUTES PREPARATION • 25 MINUTES COOKING

6 firm, medium, unblemished pears

½ lemon

1 quart (34 fl. oz/1 l red) wine

¼ cup (2 oz/60 g) superfine sugar

1 tablespoon crème de cassis

1 cinnamon stick

3 cloves

1 bay leaf

1 sprig thyme

Rind of 1 orange

1 vanilla bean

½ teaspoon fresh ground black pepper

1 Peel the pears and rub them with lemon. Put them in a saucepan. Pour in the wine and if necessary add a little water so that they are completely submerged.

2 Add the sugar, crème de cassis, cinnamon stick, cloves, herbs, grated orange rind, vanilla bean, and pepper. Bring to a slow boil and simmer for 25 minutes.

3 Remove the saucepan from the heat, take out the pears, and transfer them to a compote dish. Return the saucepan to the heat, bring the syrup back to a boil, and reduce by half before pouring over the pears.

NOUGAT GLACÉ

Iced nougat

A traditional dessert from southern France. In this recipe the chicory coulis adds an original touch. For a really smooth, rich dessert, transfer the nougat to the refrigerator for an hour before serving. Turn out onto a long dish and cut into slices.

SERVES 8 • 1½ HOURS PREPARATION

½ cup (2½ oz/75 g) raisins

1 shot glass **Grand Marnier**

¾ cup (2½ oz/75 g) blanched almonds

½ cup (2 oz/50 g) walnut halves

½ cup (2 oz/50 g) shelled pistachios

7 oz (200 g) semisweet chocolate with high cocoa-solids content

1½ sticks unsalted butter

4 medium eggs, separated

¾ cup (3½ oz/100 g) confectioner's sugar

FOR THE CHICORY/COFFEE COULIS

5 medium egg yolks

¾ cup (3 oz/80 g) superfine sugar

2¼ cups (17 fl. oz/500 ml) milk

Scant 1 cup (7 fl. oz/200 ml) whipping cream

2 tablespoons chicory extract or strong black coffee

1 Wash the raisins and soak them in the Grand Marnier.

2 Break the almonds, walnut halves, and pistachios into little pieces. Dry-roast them lightly over low heat in a nonstick skillet. Allow to cool.

3 Break the chocolate into pieces and melt with the butter in a double boiler or a heatproof bowl set over a saucepan of hot but not simmering water, then stir until smooth. Fold in the egg yolks one by one and allow the mixture to cool.

4 Put the egg whites and the confectioner's sugar in a heatproof bowl, then place the bowl over a saucepan of gently simmering water. Beat with a whisk until you have a firm and glossy meringue mixture. Mix the dried fruits and the raisins with the chocolate, then fold in the meringue mixture.

5 Turn out into a 2-lb (900-g) loaf pan lined with waxed paper and place in the freezer.

6 To make the chicory or coffee coulis, mix the egg yolks thoroughly with the sugar in a large bowl.

7 Heat the milk and cream in a saucepan. Pour the hot liquid little by little over the egg yolk mixture, stirring continuously with a wooden spoon.

8 Return the mixture to the saucepan and allow to thicken over low heat until it coats the back of the spoon. Remove the saucepan from the heat before the mixture begins to boil and add the chicory extract or coffee. Serve the coulis chilled.

DESSERTS

TARTES AUX FRAISES

Strawberry tarts

Strawberry tart is a classic dessert and a perennial favorite at Chez Serge in Saint-Ouen, France. This version is enriched with an almond cream filling, giving it a deliciously smooth texture and delicate flavor.

MAKES 4 • 25 MINUTES PREPARATION • 20 MINUTES COOKING

FOR THE FILLING

½ cup (3½ oz/100 g) sugar

1 cup (3½ oz/100 g) ground almonds

1 stick (8 tablespoons) unsalted butter, softened

1 medium egg

¾ cup (3½ oz/100 g) all-purpose flour

1 tablespoon rum or kirsch

FOR THE BASE

7 oz (200 g) puff pastry

FOR THE TOPPING

1 lb, 2 oz (500 g) strawberries

Confectioner's sugar, for sprinkling

1 Preheat the oven to 350 °F (180 °C).

2 To make the almond cream filling, mix the sugar and ground almonds together in a bowl then blend in the softened butter, egg, flour, and the rum or kirsch. Set aside in a cool place.

3 To make the base, roll out the puff pastry into four circles of the same diameter (approximately 4 inches / 10 cm). Prick the middle of each pastry circle with a fork. Spread the almond cream filling over the pastry and let sit for a few minutes.

4 Place in the oven and bake for 20 minutes.

5 Meanwhile, wash the strawberries; drain, hull, and slice thinly.

6 Take the filled puff pastry bases out of the oven and allow to cool.

7 When cool, arrange the sliced strawberries on the bases in rosette shapes. Sprinkle with a little confectioner's sugar and serve immediately.

WINE A rosé champagne

TARTE TATIN

Updside-down caramelized apple tart

One of the most famous French desserts of all, this upside-down apple tart has become a classic. The choice of fruit is important; pastry cooks recommend tart-flavored apples. Tarte Tatin can also be made with pears, quince, peaches, and other fruits.

SERVES 6 • 30 MINUTES PREPARATION • 1 HOUR COOKING

3 lb, 5 oz (1.5 kg) cooking apples

9 oz (250 g) pie dough

6 tablespoons unsalted butter

½ cup (3½ oz/100 g) sugar

1 Preheat the oven to 400 °F (200 °C). Peel and core the apples and cut them into halves. Roll out the pie dough.

2 Cut the butter into pieces and sprinkle most of the pieces evenly in a 9-inch (22-cm) round pie dish with most of the sugar. Arrange the apples on top in a rosette shape, and sprinkle the remaining sugar and pieces of butter on top of the apples. Caramelize over low heat for 30 minutes.

3 Remove from the heat and lay the pastry over the caramelized apples. Place in the oven and bake for 30 minutes.

4 Remove from the oven, place the serving dish over the pie dish, turn upside down, and serve immediately.

WINE A mellow or very sweet wine (Monbazillac, Sauternes, or Jurançon)

Tarte tatin

NOUGAT DE TOURS

Nougat, Tours style

A delicious tart, which goes very well served with tea. For a change, replace the rum with Cognac or Armagnac and the ground almonds with ground hazelnuts or coconut. Dust lightly with confectioner's sugar for an elegant presentation.

SERVES 8 • 45 MINUTES PREPARATION + 2 HOURS SOAKING • 50 MINUTES COOKING

FOR THE PIE CRUST

2¼ cups (9 oz/250 g) all-purpose flour

⅜ cup (2½ oz/75 g) superfine sugar

Pinch of salt

1 stick (8 tablespoons) unsalted butter

1 medium egg

FOR THE FILLING

½ cup (3½ oz/100 g) candied fruit, diced fine

Rum, for soaking

4 medium egg whites

1⅓ cups (4 oz/125 g) ground almonds

½ cup (3½ oz/100 g) superfine sugar

½ cup (3 oz/80 g) confectioner's sugar

1 tablespoon apricot preserves

1 To make the pie crust, blend the flour, sugar, salt, and butter together with your fingertips to obtain a powdery consistency. Then make a well in the middle and break the egg into it. Mix and knead the pastry and allow to rest in the refrigerator for 2 hours.

2 Roll out the pastry and use it to line a pie pan.

3 To make the filling, put the candied fruit in a bowl and cover with rum. Allow to soak for at least 2 hours.

4 Whisk the egg whites until stiff and carefully blend in the ground almonds, superfine sugar, and confectioner's sugar.

5 Spread a thin layer of apricot preserves over the pie crust base. Spread the drained candied fruit on top and cover with the egg white mixture.

6 Bake in a moderate oven (375 °F/ 190 °C) for 50 minutes. Serve immediately.

WINE Muscat

CRÊPES FLAMANDE

Pancakes with caramelized apples

This recipe comes courtesy of Café de Flore, in Paris. These classic French pancakes can be made with a range of sweet fillings, from a simple sprinkling of sugar and lemon juice, to wonderful mixtures of fruits and berries.

SERVES 4 • 30 MINUTES PREPARATION • 15 MINUTES COOKING

FOR THE CREPE BATTER

1 cup (4 oz/115g) all-purpose flour

Pinch of salt

1 large egg

1¼ cups (10 fl. oz/300ml) milk

1 vanilla bean

2 tablespoons unsalted butter, melted

Oil for frying

FOR THE FILLING

2 large eating apples cut into wedges

Juice of 1 lemon

1 tablespoon unsalted butter

6 no-need-to-soak dried prunes

FOR THE SAUCE

2 tablespoons butter

2 tablespoons sugar

½ cup (4 fl. oz/125ml) heavy cream

Vanilla ice cream, to serve

1 Beat together the crêpe ingredients, except for the oil which is for frying, until you have a smooth batter the consistency of light cream. Cover and refrigerate for 30 minutes.

2 Prepare a crêpe pan or skillet by heating well and wiping the surface with paper towel moistened with oil to prevent sticking. Pour in 1 tablespoon of batter and spread evenly across the pan's bottom. Cook for 1 minute, then, using a palette knife and your fingers, turn the crêpe over. Cook the other side until it is light brown. Transfer the finished crêpes in a folded cloth and place in a low oven to keep warm.

3 To make the filling, peel and core the apples, cut them into wedges, and toss in lemon juice. Melt 1 tablespoon of butter in a pan and add the apples. Cook for five minutes until just softened and lightly golden. Drain, making sure you reserve the melted butter. Set aside in a low oven to keep warm.

4 Heat the prunes in the reserved butter for a few minutes. Drain and keep warm.

5 For the sauce, heat the butter and sugar together for about 3 minutes until they caramelize. Add the heavy cream and mix until smooth.

6 Fill the crêpes with the warm fruit and drizzle with the sauce. Serve with a scoop of vanilla ice cream.

WINE Champagne

DESSERTS

TARTE À L'ORANGE ET À LA FRANGIPANE

Orange and frangipane cream tart

This tart, which can also be made with grapefruit, is filled with frangipane cream, a classic mixture of eggs, sugar, and ground almonds. In this recipe, ground hazelnuts are also added to the filling mixture. If preferred, you can replace the almonds and hazelnuts with powdered pistachios, and decorate the finished tart with crushed pistachios. If you prefer not to make your own pie dough, use $10^{1}/_{2}$ oz (300 g) ready-made pie dough or a pie shell.

SERVES 6 TO 8 • 45 MINUTES PREPARATION
$1^{1}/_{4}$ HOURS COOKING • 1 HOUR STANDING

FOR THE PIE DOUGH

$1^{2}/_{3}$ cups (7 oz/200 g) all-purpose flour

$^{1}/_{2}$ teaspoon salt

1 tablespoon superfine sugar

1 stick (8 tablespoons) unsalted butter

Grated rind of 1 orange

$^{1}/_{2}$ cup (4 fl. oz/120 ml) water

FOR THE SYRUP

3 whole oranges

$1^{3}/_{4}$ cups (14 fl. oz/400 ml) sugar syrup

Unsalted butter, for greasing

FOR THE FRANGIPANE FILLING

1 cup (8 fl. oz/250 ml) milk

$^{1}/_{2}$ vanilla bean

1 whole medium egg, plus 1 yolk

$^{1}/_{4}$ cup (2 oz/60 g) superfine sugar

$^{1}/_{3}$ cup ($1^{1}/_{2}$ oz/40 g) all-purpose flour

2 tablespoons unsalted butter

$^{1}/_{2}$ cup (2 oz/50 g) ground almonds

$^{1}/_{2}$ cup (2 oz/50 g) ground hazelnuts

1 tablespoon confectioner's sugar, to dust

Slivered almonds, for decorating

1 To make the pie dough, place the flour in a dish and make a well in the center. Add the salt and sugar. Blend in the butter in very small pieces, and the finely grated orange rind. Rub in with your

fingertips to make a crumbly mixture. Add the water a little at a time. Mix together to form a ball. The dough should be supple. Do not knead it. Wrap it in plastic wrap and allow it to rest for 1 hour in the refrigerator.

2 Meanwhile, make the syrup. Wash and brush the oranges and cut them into thin slices, discarding the pips and white lining of the orange. Place in a saucepan with the sugar syrup and the juice of the orange from which the rind was taken to make the pie dough. Allow to cook for 45 minutes, until the orange slices are transparent. Do not allow the mixture to caramelize.

3 Preheat the oven to 425 °F (220 °C).

4 Butter a 10$\frac{1}{2}$-inch (26-cm) tart pan and line it with the pie dough, rolled out into a disk shape. Prick the pie dough with a fork, cover with a sheet of baking paper, and fill with baking beans.

5 Bake blind for 10 minutes in the center of the oven then remove. Lower the oven temperature to 400 °F (200 °C).

6 To make the frangipane cream, heat up the milk with the vanilla bean. Remove the vanilla.

7 In a bowl, beat the whole egg and the extra yolk with the superfine sugar until the mixture becomes pale. Sprinkle in the flour, then pour in the warm vanilla milk.

8 Pour the mixture into a saucepan and thicken over a gentle heat, stirring constantly with a spatula without allowing it to boil.

9 Remove the saucepan from the heat, pour the mixture into a basin, blend in 1 tablespoon butter (to prevent the formation of a crust), then mix in the ground almonds and hazelnuts. Allow to cool.

10 Remove the baking beans from the pie dough and spread the frangipane cream in a smooth layer over the base of the tart. Cover with the drained orange slices, pressing them gently into the frangipane cream.

11 Dot with the remaining butter, dust with confectioner's sugar, and sprinkle over the slivered almonds.

12 Return to the oven and bake at 400 °F (200 °C) for 20 minutes. Allow to cool a little then transfer to a rack to cool completely. Serve cold.

WINE Muscat

TARTE AU CHOCOLAT

Chocolate tart

A possible variation would be to substitute crushed, roasted, unsalted pistachios for the almonds. Milk chocolate could also be used, with hazelnuts instead of the almonds, but without the orange, which goes better with semisweet chocolate.

SERVES 6 • 30 MINUTES PREPARATION • 25 MINUTES COOKING

FOR THE BASE

4 sugar lumps

1 stick (8 tablespoons) unsalted butter

2¼ cups (9 oz/250 g) all-purpose flour

FOR THE FILLING

7 oz (200 g) semisweet chocolate

½ stick (4 tablespoons) unsalted butter

⅔ cup (5 fl. oz/150 ml) crème fraîche

Handful of blanched almonds

Candied peel of 1 orange

TO SERVE

Crème fraîche

Slivers of chocolate-dipped orange rind

Unsweetened cocoa and confectioner's sugar, for dusting

1 Preheat the oven to 350 °F (180 °C).

2 To make the base, put four tablespoons water in a saucepan. Set over medium heat and add the sugar and butter. Mix well, then add the flour little by little, whisking continuously. Remove from the heat and allow to stand.

3 Line a 9-inch (23-cm) tart pan with this mixture using the palm of your hand. Place in the oven and bake for 25 minutes.

4 To make the filling, melt the chocolate gently in a double boiler, and add the butter and cream, whisking continuously. Stir briskly, remove from the heat, and allow to cool.

5 Toast the almonds under the broiler for a few minutes, taking care not to burn them. Then crush the almonds and finely dice the candied orange peel.

6 Spread the cooled chocolate cream over the base. Scatter the crushed almonds and the diced orange peel on top. Serve topped with a spoonful of crème fraîche, some slivers of chocolate-dipped orange rind, and a dusting of unsweetened cocoa and confectioner's sugar.

WINE Port or a Banyuls

DESSERTS

TARTE AUX POMMES NORMANDE

Normandy apple tart

For the people of Normandy no dish can ever have enough cream added to it. So do as they do, and serve this tart warm with a bowl of thick cream on the side.

SERVES 6 • 25 MINUTES PREPARATION • 30 MINUTES COOKING

12 oz (350 g) puff pastry

½ stick (4 tablespoons) unsalted butter, plus extra for greasing

6 tablespoons granulated brown sugar

2 medium eggs

Generous ¼ cup (1½ oz/40 g) ground almonds or hazelnuts

2¼ cups (17 fl. oz/500 ml) light cream

2 tablespoons Calvados

1 teaspoon ground cinnamon

4 firm medium apples

1 Preheat the oven to 400 °F (200 °C).

2 Roll out the puff pastry to line a 9-inch (22-cm) round buttered pie pan, and prick the base.

3 Melt the butter in a saucepan and add the brown sugar. Break the eggs in a bowl, pour over the butter and sugar mixture, add the ground nuts, and mix together. Finally stir in the cream, Calvados, and cinnamon.

4 Peel the apples, cut them into eight, and arrange them on the puff pastry base in a rosette shape.

5 Pour the mixture over the apples, making sure it doesn't come right up to the brim. Place in the oven and bake for 30 minutes.

TO DRINK Cider or Calvados

Tourtière

TOURTIÈRE

Apricot pie

Soak the apricots overnight the day before you plan to make the pie. This pie can also be made with prunes.

SERVES 6 • 25 MINUTES PREPARATION • 25 TO 30 MINUTES COOKING

9 oz (250 g) dried apricots

1 cup (8 fl. oz/250 ml) sweet white wine, such as Loupiac, Sainte-Croix-du-Mont, or Sauternes

1 tablespoon Armagnac

2 sticks unsalted butter, plus extra for buttering

1 roll phyllo pastry

1 cup (3½ oz/100 g) ground almonds

1½ tablespoons (¾ oz/20 g) sugar

Toasted slivered almonds, for sprinkling

1 The day before you plan to cook the pie, place the dried apricots in a bowl and add the wine and Armagnac. Allow to soak overnight.

2 On the day of cooking, preheat the oven to 400 °F (200 °C).

3 Drain the apricots, carefully reserving the wine. Coarsely dice the apricots. Butter a pie dish.

4 Melt the butter.

5 Brush the sheets of phyllo pastry with melted butter and arrange them one after the other in the bottom of the dish, sprinkling each sheet with ground almonds and diced apricots. Finish with a few buttered sheets of phyllo.

6 Transfer to the oven and allow to bake for 25 to 30 minutes.

7 Meanwhile, reduce the wine and the sugar in a saucepan over a low heat. When the mixture becomes syrupy, remove from the heat and allow to cool.

8 Remove the pie from the oven and pour the wine syrup over it. Serve lukewarm, sprinkled with toasted slivered almonds.

WINE A mellow or very sweet wine (Loupiac or Sauternes)